Do
YOU

Do
YOU

A Journey *of* Success, Loss, *and* Learning *to* Live *a* More MeaningFULL Life

Regina Lawless

FAST
COMPANY
Press

Fast Company Press
New York, New York
www.fastcompanypress.com

This work is being published under the Fast Company Press imprint by an exclusive arrangement with *Fast Company*. *Fast Company* and the *Fast Company* logo are registered trademarks of Mansueto Ventures, LLC. The Fast Company Press logo is a wholly owned trademark of Mansueto Ventures, LLC.

Distributed by Greenleaf Book Group

For ordering information or special discounts for bulk purchases, please contact Greenleaf Book Group at PO Box 91869, Austin, TX 78709, 512.891.6100.

Design and composition by Greenleaf Book Group and Sheila Parr
Cover design by Greenleaf Book Group and Sheila Parr
Cover concept by Jeffery Toney
Cover images © Shutterstock/Pinglabel and Analogvibestudio; © iStockphoto/ivanastar

Publisher's Cataloging-in-Publication data is available.

Print ISBN: 978-1-63908-078-6

eBook ISBN: 978-1-63908-079-3

To offset the number of trees consumed in the printing of our books, Greenleaf donates a portion of the proceeds from each printing to the Arbor Day Foundation. Greenleaf Book Group has replaced over 50,000 trees since 2007.

Printed in the United States of America on acid-free paper

23 24 25 26 27 28 29 30   10 9 8 7 6 5 4 3 2 1

First Edition

To Al, for the love we shared in this lifetime and beyond

Contents

ONE

It Was All a Dream

"I feel WILD. I used to be controlled, purposeful, and poised—but never wild. Grief has a way of unbinding you."
—MY JOURNAL, 6.20.21

On the morning of the Friday before my husband died, I had a major presentation at work and was nervous beyond belief.

It was May 21, 2021, and I was scheduled to cohost Instagram's internal Q&A with the head of Instagram, Adam Mosseri. The Q&A session is conducted in an IG Live format—only the audience consists of Instagram employees only. The night before, I had written down my talking points—*Be sure to emphasize the work we're doing to support Black women at Instagram*, I captured.

That question came up at a recent company Q&A, and I wanted to make sure I addressed it again with authority and compassion. Not only was it my responsibility to speak to this as the head of Diversity, Equity, and Inclusion (DEI) for Instagram, but I also felt a special responsibility regarding our progress for women of color as the only Black woman on Instagram's leadership team.

That morning I woke up extra early to ensure I had time to do more than my basic Zoom-worthy makeup. This event required a full face and a bold red lip! I quickly finished getting dressed and setting up the lights in my home office, giving me time to spare to run downstairs and make a cup of tea. As my tea brewed, I ran through my talking points again to make sure I could recite the key points without sounding too rehearsed.

This would be the second time I had appeared on the Instagram Q&A since I joined the company in November 2020. The first time I cohosted the event was a couple of months after I was hired. That appearance was nerve-racking as well. It was my first time being introduced to the organization as the new head of DEI. My role was created in the wake of the murder of George Floyd, and the stakes couldn't be higher to come in and make visible progress on racial equity—no pressure!

But strangely, this second appearance on Q&A felt more pressurized. Maybe it was the pent-up frustration in the organization that we weren't making enough progress, or perhaps it was me placing more pressure on myself to convey that I had everything figured out. Either way, I found myself pacing behind the island in my kitchen, feeling like I had something to prove. Once I heard the teapot's whistle, I grabbed my Instagram-branded mug (yes, I have one of those) and went back to my desk upstairs to set up my phone for the Live.

After the Q&A session was over, I felt a rush of relief. I had succeeded in sharing the key initiatives my team and I were driving to support underrepresented people at Instagram. I got to showcase more of my personality with some fun, unscripted banter with Adam and our head of Marketing, who joined the session.

That night my husband, Al, suggested we go out to eat since he knew how hard I had been working to prepare for Q&A. We went to our favorite taco truck in Brentwood and stopped by Crumbl for an assortment of cookies for dessert. It was a warm night in May, one of those perfect summer nights when the breeze was just right, and you could sit outside all night. Al and I sat in the car with all the windows down, listening to music and chatting as we waited for our food. I told him all about the Q&A, and he told me how much he was learning at his new job. Three weeks prior, he had just started at a new company to complete his externship as a sterile processing technician. He was so excited, and I was so proud of him for sticking it out and finishing his program during the pandemic so he could pursue this new career. As we sat there talking, it seemed like we had our whole lives ahead of us.

But just two days later, Al died, leaving my whole world shattered.

Time to Wake Up

I woke up that Sunday morning and knew something was wrong because Al wasn't in bed. Before he fell asleep the night before, Al told me he wasn't feeling well, but neither one of us thought much of it. It wasn't uncommon for him to have acid reflux and indigestion, which is what we assumed it was.

That Saturday morning, the day before he passed, Al woke up feeling some discomfort in his chest. I leaned over to listen to his chest and heard some wheezing that worried me, but he dismissed it as heartburn. I offered to take him to urgent care to get him checked out, but he said he'd be fine. I gave him that worried "Are you sure?" look, and he finally relented and got out of bed to grab his laptop and make a doctor's appointment for first thing Monday morning.

We lay back down and talked for a little bit, but then he was up and out of bed to walk the dog and take our fifteen-year-old son to get a haircut. It was Saturday, so I had errands to run too. I was also planning to visit my parents, who lived thirty minutes away. Out of the blue, Al asked me to wait for him.

"It's been a while since we've spent the whole day together," he said. He was right. Things had been so busy with me and my new job at Instagram and trying to stay on top of the never-ending operations of our household that we hadn't had much time to ourselves. So I waited for him to get back home, and then we headed down to Livermore to visit my folks.

We spent a couple of hours laughing and hanging out with my mom and dad, then ended up taking my mom shopping with us for some stuff I needed for the house. After dropping my mom off, I thought it was time to head back home. But Al insisted we go out to dinner and make it a real date night. It felt like old times as we sat and had a cocktail (or two) and laughed at our life over a great meal.

When we got back home, Al wasn't feeling well again. I knew he was sick because we stopped at his favorite ice cream shop before heading home, and he didn't even touch his sundae. We tried to watch a movie when we got home, but Al turned to me on the couch and said he was feeling full and uncomfortable and just wanted to lie down. So we turned off the TV and went upstairs to bed.

Shortly after we lay down, Al got up, and I could hear him in the bathroom vomiting. After a few rounds of getting out the bed to rush to the bathroom, he eventually relocated to the downstairs bathroom so he wouldn't disturb my sleep. Strangely, I wasn't too worried because it was normal for him to occasionally eat something rich and then have a bout of indigestion or vomiting.

But when I woke up that Sunday morning, a flicker of worry stirred in my stomach as I realized that Al hadn't returned to bed. I went downstairs to check on him and saw that he wasn't feeling any better and now couldn't keep any fluids down. I decided to go to the store to grab him some Pedialyte and some antacids.

When I got back to the house, Al was lying on the couch in the living room, looking flushed and weak. I went over to him to feel his forehead. He felt clammy and could barely talk. It was clear that something was really wrong and everything we tried at home wasn't working. I immediately called his doctor, thinking I could get him an urgent care appointment that morning. When the advice nurse heard Al's symptoms coupled with him being a diabetic, she told me to get him to the hospital immediately.

I hung up and called 911 and began shuffling around the house to grab Al's shoes and wallet while I read off the names and dosages of his medication to the dispatcher. When the ambulance arrived a few minutes later, I was still pretty calm because Al had gone to the hospital before for similar symptoms.

I was rushing out the garage door to follow the ambulance in my car when our son came to see us off. I told him not to worry—that everything would be okay. "Daddy and I should be back later today," I said.

But things were not, in fact, okay. And Al would never set foot back home again.

At 3:13 p.m. that Sunday afternoon, Al passed away from a heart attack, and suddenly I was a widowed mom at forty years old. I believed we had the rest of our lives together—and I had it all planned out.

* * *

I had lived my entire life up until that point with a roadmap. I knew where I was going, and Al was riding shotgun beside me. He'd had a front-row seat to every significant achievement since we met when I was eighteen. He knew I aspired to rise to the highest heights of corporate, and he encouraged me every step of the way.

I was obsessed with two things in life: my family and my career. But without Al, who was I anymore? What was my purpose? Aside from being a wife and mom, I thought it was my career. But when you lose the centerpiece of your world in an instant, nothing makes sense. Nothing seems worth living for. Not even the career I worked so hard to build from the ground up.

Follow the Yellow Brick Road

Landing the job at Instagram was the highlight of my career. In many ways, I had been working my entire career to get there, starting with my first corporate job out of college at Mervyns. This beloved Northern California-based clothing retailer has since gone out of business. I graduated from college a year prior with a bachelor's degree in communications and was returning to a full-time job after staying home to care for our infant son. It was time to get back to work, and Mervyns was the perfect place to get my corporate career started.

I was hired initially as a temporary human resources assistant. I was responsible for filing employee paperwork and scheduling appointments for the HR managers and directors. I sat at a desk at the end of a row of cubicles where the HR representatives sat. For those unfamiliar with HR, the HR representative (more commonly known as the HR business partner now) was the person assigned to be the HR contact for a particular department or function. These people answered employee questions and advised managers on all things people-related.

The HR representative role seemed so glamorous to me as I watched them sashay off with their laptops, notepads, and Blackberries in tow to meet with business leaders. They seemed powerful and well-connected, and I wanted in! I knew the role was perfect for me and was a necessary stepping stone to the position I truly coveted: HR director.

Mervyns was a significant milestone in my career. It was where I got exposure to senior leaders and realized how my role could impact so many people. It's also where I began learning to downplay and silence my needs as I grew my career.

With Al working the evening swing shift, it was on me to get home on time each weekday to pick up our one-year-old son from daycare. I would manage each minute of my day diligently to get the work done, leave a little time to socialize with my work friends, and hit the freeway by 5:00 p.m. It seemed like every time I took on a new role to grow my career—I took on a new hardship to go with it.

Over the years, it was nothing for me to leave for work before 6:00 a.m., commute one and a half to two hours to work, blaze through meetings, pick up my son from daycare, cook dinner, put him to bed, and answer work emails before I hit the bed. And those were days when I didn't have a business trip that week. Most days, Al and I were ships passing in the night, trying to survive the daily grind as a young family. By the time I joined Instagram, I had been clawing my way up the HR ladder for fifteen years and now had arrived as an executive at one of the most influential companies in the world.

When I got the job at Instagram, I was ecstatic. When the executive recruiter first reached out to me through LinkedIn, I was convinced it was a long shot despite all of my experience. I thought a company as big as Facebook would have hundreds of applicants vying for that role and couldn't possibly pick me.

I almost didn't respond to the recruiter because I doubted I would get the job. My imposter syndrome was alive and well, even at this stage in my career. My family and I were spending a few days in Half Moon Bay when I received the LinkedIn message from the recruiter. I told Al and then dismissed the idea just as quickly.

As we were sitting in the car waiting for our lunch from a local sandwich shop, Al turned to me and said, "Why wouldn't it be you?" He convinced me to respond to the recruiter, which I did as we ate lunch in the car. Roughly two months and nine interviews later, I had the job—and it was a dream come true.

At that point in my life, I felt like I had it all. I had a supportive husband. My fifteen-year-old son was growing into a wonderful young man. We owned a nice house in a quiet California suburb. I had a new Mercedes truck, the most expensive car I'd ever owned. And I had a fantastic circle of close family and friends. What more could I ask for? I had followed the established path and had finally arrived! Yet, despite having all the outward trappings of success, I was feeling deeply unfulfilled.

We Ignore the Whispers

Before the pandemic started, I routinely worked fifty to sixty hours per week and commuted no less than three hours daily for nearly ten years. But this was the price for success. The long commute was customary in the Bay Area, and as a Black woman working in corporate America, I felt I always had to be on point to avoid the perception that I didn't belong in the room.

This constant pressure to be "on" at work and the need to manage my self-image was exhausting. I would over prepare for meetings to make sure I could intelligently answer any question that came my way, despite most men in those meetings not having a problem riffing on an answer off the top of their heads. I would look at them in awe and wonder why I couldn't just spout things off with such unwavering confidence.

For most of my career, middle-aged White men were my role models at work because women and people of color in leadership were few and far between. So I tried my best to contort myself into some awkward version of me that felt like I was playing dress-up.

At one point, I was dressing for the part. I had landed a role at a regional bank—a huge opportunity to advance my career in the field of organization development, in which I had gotten my master's degree a couple of years prior. When I interviewed with the bank, it was clear how conservative they were. People wore business attire, and I encountered no Black people in the office, which made me feel that I had to represent for us all.

In preparation for my first day of work, I picked out my outfit carefully. I landed on a white blazer with a subtle pattern and black piping on the lapel, black dress pants, and a pair of black loafers with a slight wedge heel. But the real decision point was my hair.

I often wore my hair natural or in braids, but given the environment at the bank, I was worried they might not see me as professional if I didn't have my hair pulled back or straightened. So, I did what so many Black women have sadly done in the office to blend in—I tucked my curls and my cultural identity neatly underneath a wig.

The rise to executive ranks was steep, even though I followed the established playbook. Get your bachelor's degree. Check. Get a master's degree to advance into leadership. Check. Be open to relocation and business travel. Check. Be willing to take on challenging work assignments to prove yourself. Check. Always be available. Check. Never surprise your boss and always make them look good to their boss. Double check. Add in a spouse, a child or two, a home in the suburbs, a dog, and one good vacation a year, and you have the American Dream starter kit.

From the time I was a little girl, these were the things I was taught to aspire to, and I know I'm not alone. For so many of us growing up, particularly in America, we're sold this idealized dream life. We are not only supposed to sacrifice whatever it takes to get it, but we also should be grateful and happy when we achieve it.

I had achieved the American Dream and then some. I was highly paid and highly successful, but I wasn't happy. Deep down inside, I knew I wasn't being my authentic self. Too often, I would carefully couch my opinion to ensure I was liked and avoid being viewed as an "angry Black woman"—which I now know is an impossible tightrope. I learned to water down my innovative approaches to fall in line with the status quo, and I even compromised my dreams of starting my business years ago to maintain a steady paycheck to support my family.

As early as five years into my career, I began to see the toll all this working, striving, and conforming was taking on my mental health and the stress it was putting on my family. At this stage of my career, I was working for a consumer packaged goods company. I had hastily interviewed for and accepted this job all on the same day, which should have been a major red flag. However, I was desperate to get away from my existing job because after two years of excellent performance evaluations and volunteering for every assignment I could to keep proving my skills, they still hadn't promoted me to manager.

So, I took a leap into an unfamiliar industry, thinking, *How bad can it be?* Well, it turned out that it could be—and was—incredibly, unbearably bad. If you have ever seen the movie or read the books from the *Hunger Games* series, it was like that, but in an office with adults more ruthless than the fictionalized characters.

I had previously worked in places where colleagues were friendly and helped you out or at least didn't undermine you. Here, it was every person for themselves; you had to watch your back, and everything you said could and would be used against you. I felt so lost and depressed because I didn't know how to get myself out of that situation.

Some days I would drive home from work in tears. My parents taught me never to give up, but I couldn't cope in that toxic environment. I would take long lunches to get away from people in the office, and most days, on my commute to work, I would feel sick to my stomach as though I were heading for the guillotine.

At the risk of sounding overly dramatic, I felt like I was dying a little each day on the inside at that job. I believe the physical discomfort and emotional heaviness I was feeling were signs or whispers from my soul that I was not where I belonged and wasn't living in my purpose.

If you're reading this book, I imagine you have heard these whispers, too—that soft inner voice asking you, "What if?" or "What could have been," while you sit in traffic or wait in line for your coffee. We all hear these whispers from time to time—little nudges to examine the direction we're headed.

By the time Al died, I had ignored those whispers for years. I had suppressed my pain and desires so much that I was disconnected from what I truly felt and what I really wanted in life. I thought I wanted success. That is what I had been chasing my whole life. But what is success really when you lose it all in the blink of an eye?

It was clear I needed another anchor when my husband died because the life I had built now felt meaningless. And I was left floating in the wind, unrecognizable to myself.

Whose Rule Is It, Anyway?

I have experienced burnout at least three times in my career, and I was on my way back to that state at Instagram before my husband died. I was once again working myself to excess to stay on top of the success I had worked my entire career to attain. It was a never-ending hamster wheel that I didn't even realize I was on. And I know I'm not alone. In American society, burnout has become a badge of honor and an acceptable price to pay for success. In Deloitte's Women at Work 2023 survey, while burnout decreased overall from the previous year, it remains higher for women of color at 33 percent compared to 28 percent of women in the ethnic majority in their country of residence.[1]

Burnout is one of those terms often thrown around at work, but it can be hard to describe. Luckily there is an official definition. The World Health Organization (WHO) classified burnout as an "occupational phenomenon" in 2019 and defines it as a syndrome "resulting from chronic workplace stress that has not been successfully managed."[2] It is characterized by three dimensions:

- feelings of energy depletion or exhaustion
- increased mental distance from one's job, or feelings of negativism or cynicism related to one's job
- reduced professional efficacy

Do these feel familiar? Women report more feelings of burnout than men because of unequal demands at work and home that were exacerbated during the pandemic. Burnout can manifest as exhaustion, frequent headaches, gastrointestinal problems, sleep disturbances, negative attitudes, or irritability, among other symptoms. Burnout leads to more sick days and decreased performance. People suffering from burnout are three times as likely to leave their jobs.[3] This has wide-ranging effects on our companies, families, and communities—not to mention our overall quality of life.

In the wake of the global pandemic, life as we know it has

---

1   Women @ Work 2023: A Global Outlook, Deloitte, https://www.deloitte.com /global/en/issues/work/content/women-at-work-global-outlook.html.

2   "Burn-out an 'Occupational Phenomenon': International Classification of Diseases," May 28, 2019, World Health Organization, https://www.who.int/news/item/28-05 -2019-burn-out-an-occupational-phenomenon-international-classification-of-diseases.

3   "What Is Burnout? 16 Signs and Symptoms of Excessive Stress," February 27, 2021, Positive Psychology, https://positivepsychology.com/burnout/#:~:text=The%20 physical%20symptoms%20include%3A%201%20Feeling%20exhausted%20 2,problems%205%20Sleep%20disturbances%206%20Shortness%20of%20breath.

drastically changed. From the "Great Resignation" to "Quiet Quitting," workers are reconsidering their careers in the context of how they want to live their lives. Over four million women left the workforce during the pandemic.[4] The primary reason women exited is due to childcare and having to shoulder more of the responsibilities at home than men do. Climbing the corporate ladder as a woman leader before COVID-19 already required many sacrifices. Pile on remote work with few boundaries, kids out of school or daycare, and productivity demands, and you have a recipe for burnout.

For women of color, these demands can be even greater because we're often juggling additional familial responsibilities as head of the household or caretakers and providers for extended family while dodging microaggressions and lack of support in the workplace. Not surprisingly, women of color were hardest hit by the pandemic, with Black and Latina women experiencing higher rates of unemployment.[5] For those returning to the workforce, there are a myriad of barriers to overcome, including being overrepresented in low-wage service jobs and underrepresented in corporate leadership. Despite these insurmountable barriers, women of color are among the most ambitious in the workforce. For example, McKinsey cites that 59 percent of Black women leaders want to be top executives.[6] However, many of us have reached a breaking point. According to *Forbes*, one in three women of color in the workforce plan on leaving their jobs within the next year, and the top reason for leaving is burnout.[7]

---

4   Stacey Vanek Smith, "Women, Work, and the Pandemic," June 9, 2021, NPR, https://www.npr.org/2021/06/09/1004892039/women-work-and-the-pandemic.

5   *Labor Force Statistics from the Current Population Survey*, "E-16: Unemployment rates by age, sex, race, and Hispanic or Latino ethnicity," US Bureau of Labor Statistics, bls.gov.

6   *Women in the Workplace 2022*, Lean In, leanin.org.

7   Georgene Huang, "New Research Reveals 1/3 Women of Color Are Ready to Leave the Workplace by Next Year," *Forbes*, April 7, 2021, https://www.forbes.com/sites/georgenehuang/2021/04/07/new-research-reveals-13-women-of-color-are-ready-to-leave-the-workplace-by-next-year/?sh=779b44f85d4b.

The rules we've been taught, especially in marginalized communities in America, are to put your head down, work hard, sacrifice your time and energy, and that will lead to success. If we've learned anything from the pandemic, it's that these rules are broken and never have worked for everyone, especially not for women of color. But I believe there's a different way—a road less traveled that redefines success as inner peace, not outward appearances or achievement.

In the wake of my husband's death, I discovered a new way of being in the world. It began with me examining some painful feelings that I thought were long dead and buried. This initial step, to *reconnect with my heart*, was crucial in understanding what had happened to me, who I truly was inside, and what I wanted for myself moving forward.

The next step was to get back in touch with my body. I began having panic attacks just days after Al passed, so I discovered ways to calm my nervous system and *restore my body*. One of the biggest challenges to address was my mental health. Grief is a roller coaster of emotions, and I was experiencing every single one of them, especially anxiety and a profound sense of loss and disillusionment. Life was not what I believed it to be, and I had to create new beliefs; I had to *reframe my beliefs* from being a victim to being a survivor.

Another challenge I faced after Al's death was finding happiness again. In the beginning, I felt guilty for even smiling. Eventually, I learned to *renew my spirit*, which meant discovering what lights me up and brings me joy. Of course, none of this new way of being would have lasted without building new practices into my daily life. Through roughly eighteen months of trial and error, I *reinvented my routines* and went from chaos to renewed hope and sustained bliss.

The five-step process I just described was not linear, by the way. I cycled through some of these multiple times until things stuck. And speaking of stuck, I believe you're reading this book because you feel stuck in some area of your life. Maybe you've experienced a loss. Or perhaps you have it all and still find yourself longing for deeper meaning and purpose. I understand where you're coming from.

In the chapters that follow, I will share my journey to redefine success for myself and my method to discover how to live a more meaningful life:

- Reconnect with your HEART ♡
- Restore your BODY
- Reframe your BELIEFS
- Renew your SPIRIT ✳
- Reinvent your ROUTINES

And in case you think that this method may not apply to you because you haven't lost a loved one as I have, please know that loss or trauma is not required. While tragedy is often a catalyst for change, simply tapping into your inner spirit or listening to that whisper I mentioned earlier is enough to start this journey toward greater alignment and purpose.

By reading my story, in all its uncertainty and messiness, I hope you will see yourself. And my ultimate wish is that through this framework, you will come to redefine what success means uniquely for YOU and find the courage to bring the life you desire *and deserve* into glorious existence.

TWO

Unexpected Turbulence

*"Did you know pain could run this deep? I
didn't. No one explained to me that you could
be so deeply gutted in an instant."*

—MY JOURNAL, 8.22.21

I hate to fly. As much as I've traveled for work over the years, you'd
think I'd be used to it by now. Earlier in my career, I worked for an
airline called Virgin America. As an employee relations manager, I
was responsible for advising on company policies and investigating
employee complaints for our flight attendant population. I was also
assigned to support several airport locations, including San Francisco
(SFO), Los Angeles (LAX), and Chicago (ORD). I traveled often,
sometimes visiting these airports three or four times a month.

I was very familiar with being on an airplane and had even been in a
cockpit before. One of the coolest experiences I had at Virgin America
was getting the opportunity to try out the flight simulator and touch

what seemed like an endless panel of buttons, gauges, and switches that pilots must consistently monitor and operate in flight. This gave me a newfound respect for our pilots and the awesome responsibility they carried each time they took off.

Despite knowing my way around a plane, I still felt scared of turbulence. I couldn't help but wince at every dip or bump we encountered in the sky. Sometimes I would grab the armrest, while other times, I would just close my eyes and pray. Before every takeoff, prayer was a regular part of my routine. I would gently close my eyes and ask God for safe travels. I would often keep my eyes closed during takeoff until I could feel us leaving the ground. At this point, I would quietly say to myself, "Okay, wheels up." Then I could relax and peruse the magazines I always bought from the airport bookstore before my flight.

I felt at peace once I had prayed, believing I had some measure of control through my heavenly request for my plane not to fall from the sky. I had grown up in church, and prayer was something I had learned to do on a daily basis—to give thanks, ask for forgiveness, and yes, make special and sometimes unreasonable requests, like the time I asked God to clear a path for me on the freeway as I sped home to make curfew. In my understanding of the world, God worked miracles.

And that Sunday morning in May 2021, as I arrived at the hospital where my husband had just been taken by ambulance, I was about to need the biggest miracle of them all.

A Wing and a Prayer

I had arrived at the hospital in a frenzy. I couldn't keep up with the ambulance as I followed them because they were speeding with full lights and sirens, and I seemed to hit every stoplight. When I finally reached the hospital, I struggled to find parking. I drove around the building a couple of times until I discovered a side lot for visitors by the emergency room entrance. At this point, I felt like I was running late and couldn't help but feel the anxiety rising in my stomach as my heart beat a million times a minute.

I entered the waiting room and saw a sea of people. As I fidgeted nervously with my purse, I waited somewhat patiently in line despite wanting to hurdle over the desk and find Al. When I finally made it up to the receptionist, I told her my name and that my husband had just been admitted to the ER. It seemed to take her forever to look up his name as my nerves were doing backflips inside. Once she found him in the system, she told me I could come on back, where a nurse met me.

"Your husband had a heart attack," she told me.

"A heart attack?" I asked, feeling stunned as I tried to process this.

"You didn't know?" the nurse responded.

I, in fact, did not know. I had no idea and didn't know what to think or feel. She told me Al had a major heart attack in the ambulance on the way there and likely was having a heart attack when the ambulance arrived at our house.

At this point, I asked to see Al. She walked me over to him; he was lying on a gurney, barely conscious, with tubes taped to him everywhere. I immediately went to his side and grabbed his hand. He opened his eyes a little but couldn't talk.

I squeezed his hand and looked into his eyes. "I'm so sorry, babe. I didn't know it was this bad." Tears streamed down my face. He squeezed my hand and looked me in the eyes tenderly, conveying what I imagined to be *It's okay, I know.*

As the technicians rushed Al off to the cath lab, the cardiologist on duty asked me some questions about Al's medical history. We walked down what seemed like a never-ending corridor with one twist after another. The doctor asked why we hadn't come sooner, saying in what he probably thought was a comforting tone that there is a higher likelihood of survival if you get to the hospital within the first hour of a heart attack. As I swallowed my tears, I told him we didn't realize it was a heart attack. His question cut like a knife and piled on a mountain of guilt that would take months of therapy to unpack.

On the way to the hospital, I called my parents and told them that Al was sick and had been taken to the hospital. I told them there was no need for them to come just yet, but my mom insisted they'd be on their way. When I got to the cardiac waiting room, I proceeded to call Al's family, starting with his brother Karriem, with whom Al was closest. Al's mother also lived with Karriem, so I knew calling him would be the quickest way to notify everyone else in his family.

That Sunday morning, I was the only person in the small cardiac waiting room. The room had a small TV mounted high in the corner. There were four or five chairs and a small green leather bench against one wall, which is where I sat. I sat on that green bench, waiting anxiously for our family members to arrive. I texted my brother and sister to let them know the situation, but since they lived hours away, I told them not to worry yet because I believed things would be okay.

At first, I truly thought Al would make a full recovery. *How could he not?* I thought. After about an hour, a new doctor entered the waiting room to give me a status update. He told me they were doing everything they could, but things were not looking good. At that moment, the impossible crossed my mind: *Al might not make it.* I asked him if he thought I should have our son come to the hospital, and he said yes—there was no guarantee Al would make it through the night. He told me they were putting in a stint and would try to operate if they could get his heart to beat again on its own.

After the doctor left the waiting room, I lowered my head, clasped my hands, and began to pray harder than I ever had before. "Lord, please don't take my husband," I pleaded, fighting back tears. I could feel my heart racing, and the room seemed like it was spinning. *He can't die*, I thought. *He's too young. He's only forty-five! This can't be real. No, no, no, this isn't happening. Not to us. Not right now.*

I prayed for several minutes and then kept praying throughout the afternoon, as I had been taught to do all my life. I believed that if I prayed hard enough and had the faith of a mustard seed, everything would work out. After I bargained with God to let my husband live, I waited alone in that small room for my parents to arrive. *It's in God's hands now*, I thought. But I had a nagging worry in the pit of my stomach that perhaps this time, my prayers would not be fulfilled.

Through the Looking Glass

Eventually, the doctor returned and said they'd been artificially pumping Al's heart for thirty minutes and had done all they could do, but his heart just wouldn't beat on its own. I was in denial; I wasn't ready to let him go. *No, he can't be dying*, I kept saying to myself. But I knew Al wouldn't want to be kept alive on life support. We had had that conversation years earlier, so when the nurse walked over to me to say they were going to stop the machine, I swallowed hard and reluctantly said, "Okay."

By this time, Al's family had arrived, along with my parents and our son. We were all waiting in the hallway outside the tiny room where three healthcare workers had been trying to keep Al alive. I had been allowed to be in the room with him for a few minutes—holding his hand, desperately searching for signs of life. I invited our son, Morgan, into the room with me next so he could have a few minutes with his father to say goodbye. He stood quietly at Al's bedside with tears in his eyes, gently touching his dad's hand. I then embraced Morgan tightly, and we cried together, neither of us ready to let go of Al or each other.

The staff then allowed family members to go into Al's room to say goodbye. After everyone who wanted to see Al had done so, the nurse came to tell me it was time to take him off the machine. I closely watched the heart rate monitor beep . . . beep . . . beep . . . until it stopped—and then I let out a guttural scream, knowing that flat line meant the end of his life and mine as I knew it.

Leaving the hospital was a blur. I'm actually not sure how I got myself home. A few relatives offered to drive me home, but I insisted on driving myself. I wanted to be alone. I wasn't ready to talk. I didn't want to face the music. But mostly, I think I was just in shock, and I drove myself home on autopilot. By the time I arrived, our family had begun gathering at my place. My sister Kea had rushed up from Merced, about an hour and a half away. She had hastily packed an overnight bag and sped to my house, arriving disoriented from the shock. I could tell she had been crying in the car because the remnants of her tears clung to the bottom of her eyes. She came in and immediately hugged me. I clung to her fiercely as the tears rolled down my face.

Then friends, both Al's and mine, showed up to share the grief and disbelief of him being gone so soon. His best friend, Wes, was visibly in shock when he and his family showed up to comfort me. He and Al had worked together for nearly eight years and had become like brothers in that span of time. A houseful of family and friends was there to comfort my son and me, which in hindsight, is exactly what we needed at that moment—especially since both of us tend to retreat and bury our feelings.

I stayed downstairs to talk to people for as long as I could, knowing that I didn't want to go to sleep. Part of me was still in shock, running on adrenaline, so I wasn't feeling tired yet. But another part of me knew that if I went to sleep, I would wake up tomorrow without my husband. This was a reality I wasn't ready to face, so I kept awkwardly chatting with my loved ones until my sister-in-law Nicole volunteered to stay the night with us and finally convinced me to go to bed. Eventually, I cried myself to sleep. When

I woke up around 6:00 a.m. the next morning, I was in an alternate universe where my husband didn't exist. I was floating outside my body, stuck in between time.

Everyone seemed to be concerned about me and was equally attentive to Morgan. All things considered, my son was holding up fairly well despite losing his father at the pivotal age of fifteen. What they say about kids being more resilient than adults is true.

I, on the other hand, was a total mess, a listless shell of my former self. As time went on, most days, I still got up early as I had been conditioned to do for years. But I had to force myself to get out of bed. If it weren't for my dog, an adorable Shih Tzu-poodle mix named Rocket, who was accustomed to his morning walks with my husband, I probably wouldn't have gotten out of bed at all. Each day it felt like I was wading through quicksand; my life as I knew it was dissolving beneath my feet.

Rocket forced me out of bed each morning, but my family kept me going. The first two weeks after Al died, I was always surrounded by family. My mother came by and called to check on me every morning. My father called to check on me and sent scriptures. Al's brother, Karriem, and his wife, Nicole, checked in consistently and brought over meals, and countless other family, friends, and work colleagues enveloped us in food, flowers, prayer, and love.

A few days after Al passed, my younger brother Mark arrived with his wife and daughter to grieve with us and help in any way leading up to the funeral. Having my brother and his family, my sister, and my son under one roof would have felt like an old-school sleepover if the circumstances weren't so devastating.

Those first two weeks were a blur because I had so many quick yet lasting decisions to make about where to hold Al's funeral service and how best to honor his memory. The frenzy of it all kept me in a suspended state of disbelief. But once the funeral was over and most of my family had gone home, I had no choice but to face myself.

And Still, I Rise

Al's death took everything I knew to be true about life and flipped it on its head. Before Al's death, I was the type of person who believed that bad things happened to bad people. I naively thought I was immune to tragedy because I followed the rules, was kind to people, and did good deeds. I have always been empathetic to others when something terrible happened, but I thought those things couldn't happen to me. I worked so hard to get an education, advance in my career, and build a nice life for myself. But none of those things shielded me. Tragedy blew up my life anyway.

Existential thoughts ran through my head on a loop as I struggled to make sense of it all.

> *How could this be happening to me?*
> *Why me?*
> *What did I do wrong?*
> *Why would God take my best friend and partner away in an instant?*
> *I didn't even get a chance to say goodbye.*
> *How am I supposed to go on?*
> *What am I going to do with the rest of my life?*
> *Who am I anymore without him?*
> *Why didn't I call 911 sooner?*
> *This was all my fault.*
> *I should have done more to save him.*

I was drowning in my thoughts. The mental anguish was torture. But grief also takes a physical toll on your body that feels excruciating. Most days, I woke up like I had been in a fight, feeling sore and exhausted. My nervous system was so on edge that I had to find activities I hadn't done since I was a kid, like painting and doing puzzles, to focus my mind and steady my heart rate. These activities also helped to temporarily take my mind off my grief and the overwhelm of it all. For those first few weeks and months, I felt totally out of control—completely disconnected from reality and the life I had known.

I was a person who always had a plan. I used to plan parties for my Barbie dolls as a kid. I planned school dances as a member of the student body leadership in middle school. I planned our music and dance routines as captain of my high school dance troupe. I planned to finish college, get married, start a family, and live happily ever after. And even when I encountered a setback, of which there were many, I didn't get too bummed because I always had a plan B. But when Al died so suddenly, it was a scenario I hadn't even fathomed and therefore had no contingencies in mind. I felt rudderless. There was no plan in place this time. I would have to embark into the unknown and make things up as I went along. Yikes!

The only thing I knew instinctually at first was to have some semblance of a routine. For me, that was walking Rocket every morning. At first, I resented this task. I didn't even want to get out of bed, but after the first few weeks, I recognized that getting some fresh air and sun on my face in the mornings was a blessing in disguise. It also served as time for me to process. I started to contemplate the meaning of life and question the things I had always known to be true. For instance, if terrible things can happen in an instant, does that mean there's no way to guard against them? Is there really no defense against the worst? Is life sometimes just outside of our control? How terrifying! What does that mean for someone like me who has always tried to take charge of her life and override the system to guarantee success? What if I was never in control, to begin with?

In addition to these thought-provoking morning walks, I also sought individual therapy. Ironically, I found a new therapist weeks before Al died. I hired her to deal with work stress and childhood emotions I had long ago buried, but our early sessions now shifted to my grief. Those first few sessions were lifesaving for me. The days, hours, and minutes leading up to Al's death replayed in my mind on a twenty-four-hour loop of misery. I couldn't think of anything else, yet it brought overwhelming feelings of grief, loss, anger, guilt, fear, anxiety, and many more confusing emotions that I didn't understand, let alone know how to process. Through intensive therapy sessions and EMDR (Eye Movement Desensitization and Reprocessing) techniques, my therapist helped me revisualize those traumatic moments in ways that soothed my pain and made the memories less triggering.

Even though therapy was helping me to process and cope, grief still takes time to integrate. I had learned to function but remained in a daily fog of depression for nearly eight months. I was a shell—walking, talking, and going through the motions of life but not truly feeling or being. It would be many months before friends and family told me they could see the sparkle return to my eyes.

Once I started to feel more like myself, I reflected on what had shifted in me and realized that I had been doing tiny things to help myself each day. I started with small acts of self-care, like deciding to take a shower and get dressed. Some days I found comfort in listening to a podcast on spirituality or going out for a cup of my favorite coffee. Reading, journaling, and meditating were other ways I slowly began to embrace my new reality. I wish I could say I had some grand strategy for healing, but the truth is I was as lost as you'd expect anyone to be who lost it all at once. I simply took one day—and sometimes one hour—at a time. I took my cues from my rediscovered inner voice and gradually rebuilt a beautiful life.

And *that* is the central premise of this book: Space plus time plus intention plus YOU equal the key to what I call a meaning-FULL life. And what is a meaningFULL life? Simply put, it's living a bolder life aligned with the dreams and purpose you were uniquely created for. We can all live a fuller, more meaningful life or rebuild our lives from the rubble in the image we desire. It does, however, require *space* to think and process what's on your **heart**; *time* to heal your **body**, uncover your limiting **beliefs**, and reshape your mindset; courage to live from your **spirit**; and *intention* to practice some new daily **routines** for *YOU* to bring this new life into existence. I AM LIVING PROOF.

As you're beginning to understand, I've had no easy journey. I survived the loss of my spouse—the loss of my world, really—with no clue on how to move forward. But moving forward is what I did, one painful step at a time. I kept moving forward and willed the beautiful and blissful life I have today, my meaningFULL life, into being.

And I believe you have the capacity to do this, too, my love. The rest of this book will serve as your guide. Each chapter that follows unfolds my **MeaningFULL Life Method** (*reconnect with your heart, restore your body, reframe your beliefs, renew your spirit,* and *reinvent your routines*) that came together for me through my relentless pursuit of healing and daily trial and error.

A word of caution, though. Sometimes we feel like we must overhaul our lives in an instant. I've certainly been there. There were points in my life when I was unsatisfied and wanted everything to change, but quickly became discouraged because I wasn't ready to burn everything I had worked for to the ground and start over. Don't fret—put down the matches, girl! No need to burn it all down. **I have learned through my journey that it is much more effective to allow for trial and error and make small changes over time**.

For me, the road to my meaningFULL life started with getting my emotions in check because I realized I couldn't move forward in life if I remained saddled with grief and guilt. So, I had my work cut out for me. Unearthing the emotions I had deeply buried was one of the first challenges I had to overcome to heal my heart.

THREE

Strong Black Woman

"I just want the world to stop. I want to lay down in the street and weep until my tears water the earth."

—MY JOURNAL, 6.5.21

As I walked to the podium to deliver Al's eulogy, there was a fifty/fifty chance my knees would buckle. From the front pew where I was sitting to the podium at the front of the chapel seemed like a thousand steps. I clutched my typed copy of the eulogy tightly and took one steady step at a time.

From the podium, I could see a congregation of heartache. I slowly made eye contact with as many people as I could to try to draw strength. I looked at my parents, whose sorrow was palpable. I peered over at Al's mom, whose vacant stare was the window into her broken heart. Finally, I glanced at my son sitting in the front row with my mom and dad. He looked back at me, so I knew I had to be strong for him.

When I was preparing the eulogy the week prior, a few family members asked me if I was sure I wanted to do it because they thought it would be too hard for me. I knew it would be hard, but I also knew that there was no one better than me to give the eulogy. Al and I spent twenty-one years of our lives together. No one knew him as intimately as I did. Besides, I couldn't think of a better way to honor him than to tell the story of our lives.

As I prepared to speak, I tapped the mic to make sure it was on and took my mask off so folks could hear me. I had to make one final adjustment to my hat. I was wearing a beautiful fascinator with a black bow, mesh veil, and feathers that I'd bought from the Berkeley Hat Company. I figured if I was going to get up in front of everyone and bare my soul, I might as well look fabulous doing it.

It was time to speak. I smoothed out the folded pages of my speech on the podium, gripped the mic, cleared my throat one last time, and spoke from the bottom of my heart. Once I got a few shaky words out, I knew I would be okay. My "gift to gab," as my dad liked to say, and being enveloped by all the love in the chapel that day shored up my spine to stand there and do the hardest thing I'd ever done: eulogize my other half.

After the eulogy, a parade of family and friends came up to share their stories of how Al impacted their lives. One friend spoke of Al's generosity and shared how Al was his supervisor and had given him a second chance when he should have been fired, which inspired him to be a better man. As you might expect, there wasn't a dry eye in the house.

After the service, one of my girlfriends came over to hug me. She whispered in my ear, "You're the strongest woman I know. I don't think I could have done that." "You're so strong" became a familiar refrain in the days, weeks, and months following Al's death. "I don't know how you do it" was another one. However, these compliments struck me as odd because I had no choice but to be strong. I literally knew no other way to exist in the world.

I was raised by my parents and society to be a "strong Black woman," which often meant suppressing my pain and getting on with life. My earliest example of this was my mother. I remember when my grandmother died. I was seventeen at the time, and my mom called me at work to come home because Grandma Berniece had passed away. My mom was extremely close with her mother. Yet when she passed away, my mom did not break down. She wasn't inconsolable like you see in the movies. She, of course, shed tears at the funeral, and I suspect she cried behind closed doors. But she did not allow my brother and me to see the rawness of her pain. She tried to be strong for us.

My mother, like the generations of Black women before her, was taught to be strong no matter what. Black women are encouraged to be strong, self-sacrificing, and free of emotion. In a word: superwoman. As Nichomi Higgins describes in her book *Purposeful Perspectives*, this image generally manifests as "an inherent sense of duty to take on the world and all its problems while juggling our Blackness and womanhood."[8]

This conditioning developed as a way to cope with the stress of racism and sexism Black women faced in their daily lives.[9] In the context of slavery and racial segregation, with Black women sitting at the intersection of discrimination based on race and gender,[10] it's understandable why we would need to become, on the surface, impervious to it all. Being a "strong Black woman" is a survival

---

8   Nichomi Higgins, LMFT, *Purposeful Perspectives: Empowering Black Women Towards Spiritual Alignment, Self-Mastery & Joy* (Chino, CA: Solcentered Family Therapy Inc, 2021).

9   Amani M. Allen, "Racial Discrimination, the Superwoman Schema, and Allostatic Load: Exploring an Integrative Stress-Coping Model among African American Women," The New York Academy of Sciences, August 12, 2019, https://nyaspubs .onlinelibrary.wiley.com/doi/epdf/10.1111/nyas.14188.

10 Kimberlé Crenshaw, "Demarginalizing the Intersection of Race and Sex: A Black Feminist Critique of Antidiscrimination Doctrine, Feminist Theory, and Antiracist Politics," University of Chicago Legal Forum, Vol. 1989: Iss. 1, Article 8, http://chicago unbound.uchicago.edu/uclf/vol1989/iss1/8.

technique. As a Black woman raised by a Black woman born into Jim Crow segregation in the 1950s, my mother's armor was naturally handed down to me.

I've had to be strong for as long as I can remember. When things didn't go my way, like a test or a schoolyard crush, I was taught to suck it up and move forward. Even being picked on at school became a lesson in forgiveness and grace. One incident stood out for me when I was in the second grade. Three boys from my class were bullying me because of my dark skin tone. I was so upset that I went home and told my mom. She immediately called the school principal. That same week, my mom went to my school to meet with the principal. To my surprise, Principal Knight called all three boys into her office with my mom and me present and made them apologize—after giving them a stern reprimand.

Although I basked in the sweet revenge of seeing those knuckleheads sweat, I was still hurt to the core. I thought these boys were my friends, yet they made me feel like something was wrong with me based on the color of my skin. What was even more puzzling was that two of the boys picking on me had dark skin as well. I learned then that it was only undesirable to be a dark-skinned girl. It was the first time I felt a measure of shame for simply being who I was.

But my mom told me not to let them get to me. She told me I was beautiful and to pay them no mind. She was right, yet I still had a ball of unexpressed feelings. We never unpacked my feelings about the incident, though. My only option back then was to smile and play on. So, I was back at the playground the next day, running around with those boys and pretending nothing had happened.

Emotional Ice Cap

By the time Al died, I had become so disconnected from my emotions that I didn't even know how to acknowledge, let alone feel, that level of pain. Once the funeral was over, I had to face my new normal, and I was doing an abysmal job of getting a grip. I woke up each day feeling hazy like I was living in a dream. I struggled to eat anything despite my refrigerator bursting at the seams with leftover food and my freezer filled to the brim with frozen meals my friends had delivered. I hated checking the mail and seeing envelopes addressed to Al that he would never receive. Suddenly my house felt unfamiliar to me, although we had lived there for eight years. The colors on the wall seemed dull as if someone had put monochrome glasses over my eyes. Those first few weeks, I often stared at the front door, longing desperately for Al to walk through it again. False hope seemed easier than facing the reality that the person I had spent the last twenty-one years of my life with had ceased to exist.

About a month after Al passed, my sister, Kea, moved in with Morgan and me. She was preparing to start grad school at the University of San Francisco and needed to move back to the Bay Area, so I invited her to stay with me. I had a spare bedroom and knew she needed a change of scenery.

Kea's arrival turned out to be a godsend on many levels. In the month before she arrived, I could be found lying on the couch in an almost catatonic state with the blinds closed while Morgan kept to himself in his room. I would check in with him a few times a day to make sure he was okay and then recede into darkness. When Kea came to live with us, the house was cold, dark, and lifeless. Slowly but surely, her attention and care helped breathe life back into it.

She also helped me with so many of the tasks around the house I had come to rely on Al for, like cooking. Al was an amazing cook. I, on the other hand, am an uncoordinated disaster in the kitchen, which my sister quickly helped to mitigate.

Kea was born when I was fourteen years old. For her entire life, I had been the big sister looking out for her. And now, in a beautiful role reversal, she was here taking care of me in my biggest time of need.

When I look back now, those first couple of months after Al passed are a blur. Perhaps my mind walled off the agony of those early days to spare me. What I do remember is the constant check-ins from family members, coworkers, and friends. My days were filled with calls, text messages, and deliveries. Everyone wanted to know how my son and I were holding up. And no matter who asked, I would always respond with some variation of "I'm doing okay" or "We're hanging in there." My empty stare and unkept appearance said otherwise. I just didn't know how to bring myself to say, *I'm dying over here! How do you think I'm doing?* Instead, I began to journal my feelings. Journaling was the first crack in my emotional levee. It began with me writing notes to Al on my iPhone.

> *6.5.21—I miss you. Today is two weeks since you passed away, and I miss you immensely. I can't help but think about all the things we were supposed to do this summer, let alone the rest of our lives. I had a surprise planned for your birthday. I booked a hotel room for us in Carmel. I was looking forward to surprising you after you got off work. I still can't believe you're gone. It seems like a horrible dream. A cruel and tormented joke. I keep imagining you away on a business trip and coming home any day now. But you won't. You'll never walk through those doors again, and I'll never be the same.*

I began writing messages like this every day, sometimes in my phone and other times on a notepad by my bed. When emotions started to well up in my chest, and my feelings had nowhere else to go, I wrote them down. This gave me a way to make sense of what I was going through simply by acknowledging it to myself.

Another emotional breakthrough came from an unlikely source. Up until this point, I had been on bereavement leave from work. Meta, the parent company of Instagram, has a generous bereavement leave policy of twenty-one days—essentially a month—for the death of a spouse. I was nearing the end of bereavement leave and planning to come back in late June. I had notified my direct manager that I planned to return on June 21, nearly one month after Al passed.

That week I received a text message from Adam Mosseri, the head of Instagram, checking in on me. He said he heard I was coming back soon and wrote something that caught me off guard. He texted, "Psyched to have you back, but also, please take all the time you need."

"Please take all the time you need" pierced my soul like a slingshot.

Until Adam said that, it had not occurred to me to take more time off, even though I could barely function most days. Without his subtle permission to take the time I needed, I most certainly would have done what I had been conditioned to do my whole life—stuff down my anguish and grief and keep moving. To this day, I'm so grateful for his text and that I finally had the good sense to listen. I applied for a leave of absence the next day and set my mind to using that summer to heal.

Summer of Soul

That first summer after Al passed was the bellwether of my healing journey. Once I decided to take more time off, the pressure and anxiety of having to put on a face of normalcy and return to work so soon was lifted. I could finally disconnect and figure out what came next.

Earlier that year, Al and I had planned to drive down to Southern California for the Fourth of July. My brother and his wife had just bought a home there, and we planned to help them get settled. The trip was still planned, but I wasn't sure if I had the strength to go without him. But I knew Al would have wanted me to still go, and I figured I could use some time out of the house and some love and laughter with my family.

On the Fourth of July weekend, my son, Rocket, and Kea packed our bags and headed down to Riverside County. The four of us were now a family unit, learning to navigate our collective grief of losing Al in our own unique ways. I knew this trip to LA would be good for all of us.

When we arrived at my brother's house, it felt a bit surreal for me to be there without Al. I remember Al telling me how he was looking forward to having a beer with my brother and welcoming him into the blessing and burden of home ownership. He also couldn't wait to spend time with our four-year-old niece. She adored her "Uncle Owl"—her adorable mispronunciation of his name. Al's absence was glaring. But we quickly dove into action to help my brother and sister-in-law finish their move, which was a welcomed distraction to ease my mind.

One day during our trip, we decided to visit San Diego and spend a day at the beach. It was a beautiful July day with no clouds in sight. The weather was perfect. We had come prepared for the sun with our beach shade, a cooler full of drinks, our chairs, and a portable speaker. This was my niece's first time at the beach since she could walk. She was in awe of the water but wasn't sure what to do with all the sand. Rocket, on the other hand, was an old pro.

Al and I had introduced Rocket to the beach in Half Moon Bay, and he had loved it ever since. I sat back in my chair under the shade and watched my niece explore the water with her mom and dad while Rocket chased the tide. Kea sat in a beach chair next to me, providing our soundtrack from her portable speaker. And Morgan had claimed his spot in the shade under the tent, watching the waves like me— time seemed to stand still. I continued to chill with my sunglasses on, and my head tilted to the sky, realizing this was the first moment of peace I had enjoyed in a while.

The trip to LA was good for my soul. It gave me some much-needed time with my family. To my surprise, it was also an outlet for my grief. We stayed up late talking most nights and reminiscing about the many hilarious memories we had of Al. He was so funny! We laughed for hours as we retold stories of him, including the time he ate a dog biscuit that my brother accidentally left on the kitchen table—a story that still cracks my brother up to this day.

Before this trip, I memorialized Al in private, preferring to wallow in my pain alone and crying myself to sleep every night. And I was still acting out my well-rehearsed "strong Black woman" storyline. Even when I talked about Al and shared how I felt, I still held back, despite my brother and sister-in-law embracing me with so much love. They were there with open arms and empathetic shoulders to lean on, but I didn't know how to truly open up. As close as I am to my brother, it was hard for me to be the one who needed help. I was the big sister and was supposed to be the one he could depend on. But now I needed him and everyone else to hold me up. However, I wasn't ready for the trust fall.

I told myself I had to hold it together and be strong, no matter what. I also had to hold it together for Morgan. My number one job, or so I thought, was to make sure he was okay, and his sixteenth birthday was fast approaching.

Al passed away on May 23, 2021, just two weeks shy of his forty-sixth birthday and six weeks prior to Morgan turning sixteen. I decided to throw Morgan a nice birthday party so he could celebrate with his friends. Deep down, I hoped this act of normalcy would temporarily take his mind off the loss of his dad.

Morgan loves cars, and the latest movie in the *Fast and Furious* franchise had just premiered. I thought it would be cool to rent out one of the small theaters for a private viewing for him and his friends. That idea turned out to be a hit! I also invited some family and a few friends of mine with kids to tag along.

When we arrived at the theater, I was careful not to sit too close to Morgan so he could have some space to be himself with his friends. I happily took my seat at the back of the theater with the rest of the "old heads"—a term he had gotten from his father and now jokingly applied to anyone over forty.

Morgan and his crew of friends were in the front row, laughing and carrying on like you'd expect a group of teenagers to do. I couldn't help but smile. It was the first time I'd heard him laugh since the funeral. At that moment, I let out a subtle exhale as I realized that, without a doubt, he would be okay.

After visiting my brother, it was clear that I wasn't okay and needed some more time with myself to process everything I was feeling. Before I could expose my wound to daylight, I had to learn to open it up to myself. I had thought about taking some time away not long after Al passed, but I wasn't sure I wanted to go off somewhere by myself. However, the trip to Los Angeles strengthened me. While I loved being surrounded by family, that visit reinforced my need to be alone with no one to distract me from my heartache. So, the week after Morgan's birthday party, I set off for a three-day solo stay on the Mendocino coast of California.

Mendocino is about a three-and-a-half-hour drive from my home in the Bay Area. Its situated 154 miles from San Francisco along the Pacific Ocean and is most notable for its coastal views and centuries-old redwoods. My mom tried to talk me out of my trip. "You shouldn't go up there by yourself," she told me. But I was adamant that I needed this time away . . . alone.

I hadn't had a day to myself since the funeral or a space free from constant memories to decompress. *This would be good for me*, I thought. Plus, I needed to learn to do things on my own. After all, I was now uncoupled against my will and having to fend for myself as an adult for the first time. This trip was a test of sorts—a coming out—to see if I could navigate my new life alone.

The drive up to Mendocino was gorgeous. It started out routine. From where I live in the East Bay, I had to drive almost an hour through the North Bay to Santa Rosa before heading into the mountains. I cruised along 101, singing along to my music, when the sign finally came up for 128 West to Fort Bragg. I began the winding road up through the mountains toward the Pacific coast.

There were a couple of times during my route when someone passed me on the narrow two-lane highway. But I didn't mind. I was taking my sweet time. I was slowly winding down the narrow road, one sharp turn after another. The sun was shining through the trees, and *Songs in A-Minor* by Alicia Keys was blaring through my speakers as I remembered how much I loved that album when it first came out.

I knew instantly I was close to Mendocino when I smelled the brisk, salty air. My front windows were down, and the sunroof was slightly opened, so the breeze hit me before I could even see the ocean. This part of the drive had always been my favorite. It's the point when you reach Highway 1 and begin to head down toward the coast through the redwoods. The view is breathtaking, and the redwoods are magical. It's hard to believe something has been on Earth that long and still standing, mostly undisturbed.

I started to get anxious at this point, knowing I was so close. I began to second-guess myself. *What the hell am I doing all the way up here by myself? What am I going to do for three days alone?* I could feel the anxiety stirring in my chest like bees in a hive. I took a few deep breaths as I got close to the hotel where I would be staying. Then I whispered to myself, *You've got this*. I didn't know how this trip would go, but I knew I had been strong for too long and needed a break.

The next morning, I woke up naturally with the sun peeking through the floor-to-ceiling shades that ran the length of my room. I eagerly hopped out of bed to open the shades before stepping onto the balcony. I stood there for several minutes, taking in the gorgeous view of the Pacific Ocean.

I needed to sit outside and soak it all in. I made myself a cup of coffee, grabbed a blanket, and sat on the red-stained Adirondack chair with my journal, admiring the trees, the birds, and the waves. *What a blessing to be here*, I thought. I couldn't stay wound up if I tried. And without any effort on my part, the heaviness of my grief started to wash away like the tide.

By my third day at the Heritage House Resort, I had fully settled in. At first, it was so strange being there by myself. I was easily triggered by the sight of other couples enjoying their meals together or taking a walk along the trail behind my room. It was impossible to forget that I was there alone because my husband had died. But on day two, I decided that it was only right that I make the best of it.

From then on, I was determined to make the rest of my trip about pampering myself and doing the things I liked. I went shopping. I took a nature walk along the Mendocino Coast Trail. I took myself to lunch. And I scheduled a deep tissue massage. I left the massage thinking *I could get used to this!*

By the third day, I was fully relaxed. I looked forward to staying in my room that night since I had to pack up and leave the next morning. Unfortunately, I had run out of things to eat in my room and was forced to make a trip out. Before I came to the conclusion that I would have to get dressed again, I tried several alternatives. I called the hotel to see if they offered room service, but they had stopped doing so during the pandemic. Then I called the restaurant in the hotel next door, but that was reserved for their hotel guests. I even tried to see if I could have some food delivered. All my plans fell through, so I was destined to leave the comfort of my room. Ugh!

There weren't a lot of food options without having to drive fifteen minutes to downtown Mendocino or even further up the coast to Fort Bragg. Then I remembered a French restaurant my masseuse had recommended: the Ledford House, five minutes down the road in Albion. I had been warned that the restaurant could get busy, and reservations were recommended. But I decided to head there anyway to see if I could get a table.

When I walked inside, sure enough, there were no empty tables, but the hostess said I could sit at the bar. I took her up on that offer, despite not really wanting to sit next to anyone and chat. Luckily, the bar wasn't packed. The hostess sat me next to an older woman who appeared to be finishing her meal along with her second martini. She leaned over and began making small talk. She was enjoying herself and her martini. I clearly needed to catch up to her!

I ordered a glass of Pinot Noir and stared out the window behind the bartenders, mesmerized by the golden horizon atop the ocean. *This isn't so bad*, I thought. My meal arrived, and it was even tastier than I expected. In the meantime, a couple had been seated next to me at the bar. We exchanged small talk while I ate my dinner. It wasn't long before another person joined us at the bar.

A tall, slender man with gray hair walked in and sat to my right on the corner of the bar facing me. At first, I was hoping he would keep to himself. I was enjoying the moments of silence and didn't want to get sucked into another conversation if I could avoid it. But after watching him engage with the folks around him, he seemed like a nice enough guy. So I casually said hello. He said hello in return, and for the next thirty minutes or so, Robert and I discussed everything from our children and our jobs to politics and travel, including our respective experiences of visiting India. It was a fascinating conversation.

At some point during our discussion, Robert asked me what had brought me there for dinner. I decided to share with him that my husband had died two months prior, and I planned this trip to Mendocino to rest and recover. I'm not sure what compelled me to tell all of this to a complete stranger. I guess he made me feel comfortable enough to be vulnerable in that way.

As it turned out, my vulnerability was the invitation Robert needed to discuss *his* grief. After offering his heartfelt condolences,

Robert shared with me that his wife had been paralyzed in 2010 after surgery for a brain tumor. He was dining alone at the Ledford House because his wife was too sick to join him that night. This was their spot. They had been coming to the Ledford House for dinner since the 1980s.

Just then, another person entered the restaurant and sat at the bar between Robert and me. She immediately said hello, so we naturally looped her into the conversation. We learned her name was Emily, she lived in Sonoma County, and coincidentally like Robert, she was a therapist. With Emily there, our conversation returned to travel before pivoting to social justice and mental health reform. We sat at the bar, drinking our cocktails and laughing with one another as the time effortlessly passed.

We all seemed to be enjoying the lively conversation. Robert proceeded to ask Emily what brought her to the restaurant that night. Perhaps she, too, could sense the comfort or vulnerability in the air. Whatever the cause, Emily decided to open up. She shared with us that she had just separated from her husband and, similar to me, was in the area on a solo vacation to figure things out. She and I looked at each other tenderly before exchanging condolences for what we had lost.

The three of us continued our conversation while we waited for Emily's meal to come out. I noticed the bar starting to thin out, and the sun was setting, which was a signal for me to get back to my room before it was too dark. As we were wrapping up and waiting for our checks, Emily commented that our conversation had taken her mind off her life's problems for a little while. I agreed. The whole time I sat there talking with the two of them was time I wasn't consumed by my sadness or lost in my thoughts.

But the real lesson for me was discovering for the first time since Al died that I wasn't alone in my pain. There were others navigating their own losses in the midst of living. Robert, Emily, and I were three strangers brought together that night by fate to help ease our personal suffering. Had I decided to stay in my room and not go with the flow of circumstances, I would have missed out on that encounter and its true purpose—to catalyze my healing. I drove away from the restaurant in awe, feeling more understood than I could have imagined and less alone in the universe.

Whole Black Woman

My experience in Mendocino led me to rethink how I was showing up in my grief. After journaling about my special dinner with Robert and Emily, I realized that my willingness to be open and vulnerable and hold space for others led to all of us becoming an unlikely support system for one another. I began to wonder what would happen if I honored that instinct more in daily life. I started to consider what it would look like to put down the mask and cape of the "Strong Black Woman" and simply be raw, present, and in the moment. This, of course, is so much easier said than done. I'd have to battle decades of conditioning and generations of trauma informing what it means to be a Black woman in America.

Letting go of the "Strong Black Woman" stereotype meant disentangling a core part of my identity and fighting back against firmly ingrained societal expectations. As Seanna Leath explains in her research on Black women's mental health, "Black women are required to respond to life's hardships by portraying strength and concealing trauma."[11] We are routinely praised for our strength, our caretaking abilities, and our capacity to outwork others. But, according to Leath's study of college-aged Black women, "emotional displays of vulnerability, anger, and sadness were often met with resistance" from their own family members.

---

11 Seanna Leath, "How the Expectation of Strength Harms Black Girls and Women," Scholars Strategy Network, August 15, 2019, https://scholars.org/contribution/how -expectation-strength-harms-black-girls-and.

As Leath uncovered, this conditioning to be strong at all times usually starts at home and is further reinforced for Black women at church, in our communities, and at work. Nichomi Higgins describes parts of the "Strong Black Women's Code of Conduct":

- Present an image of strength at all times and resist the expression of vulnerability unless in grief.

- Push through emotional and psychological discomfort. "Suck it up."

- Work hard without complaint. "Be grateful that you have a job."[12]

I knew I couldn't fully dismantle the superwoman stereotype or discount how deeply engrained it was in my psyche. However, I was worn down and ready to be a fuller version of myself—not a straw woman of unrealistic strength with no access to fragility, emotional depth, or peace. I wanted to be whole. To do that, I had to release the power of the "Strong Black Woman" persona and its regulation of my existence.

The summer of 2021 taught me some valuable lessons on how to lean into my emotions and simply let them be without restraint or judgment. My husband's funeral taught me that I can always rely on my well of strength like I did to deliver his eulogy, but now I also realize that this strength doesn't have to define me.

Relaxing on the beach in San Diego that summer helped me to realize the relief even an hour in the sun can bring. Journaling my thoughts helped me to tap into my deepest feelings and claim them as my own. As the adage goes, you have to feel in order to heal. Keeping a journal has been instrumental in my healing.

And my trip to Mendocino taught me to let go and trust the

---

12 Higgins, *Purposeful Perspectives.*

universe to put me right where I need to be to grow. It's these expe-riences and daily practices like journaling that finally gave me access to and comfort with my full range of emotions. Once I had a better handle on those emotions, I could sense that my body was the next warning light in need of a tune-up.

FOUR

Out-of-Body Experience

"I don't feel like doing life anymore. Life can do me.
It's already done me in fact. It's left me shattered
in a thousand pieces scattered to the wind."

—MY JOURNAL, 9.26.21

When I was seventeen years old, I enlisted in the United States Army Reserve. Although both my parents worked hard enough to catapult us into a middle-class life in the suburbs, they still couldn't save enough to pay for me to go to college. I saw the army as an opportunity to help cover my tuition, plus I had an aunty who was in the army, which made the prospect of going less scary.

By the time I graduated high school in the spring of 1999, I had orders to report to Fort Jackson, South Carolina, for boot camp that July. Prior to shipping off for boot camp, I had tried to get myself into better physical shape. As a lifelong extrovert, I used PE class for socializing, not strength training. After barely surviving a mile-long

run around my high school track, I knew I had my work cut out
for me.

Those first few weeks of physical training in the army, or PT as
we referred to it, were brutal. Each day we were required to wake up
at 4:00 a.m. for a 4:30 workout that lasted at least an hour. That, of
course, wasn't the end, though. During the course of the day, we did
everything from combat to weapons training in the hot sun, with a
jog or "double-time" walk in formation everywhere we went.

And on any given day, any drill sergeant I encountered could
order me to drop and give them push-ups, just because. Although
being ambushed with exercise is never fun, this constant physical
exertion was necessary to pass the physical exam, which was one of
the final requirements to graduate boot camp.

After nearly nine weeks of army boot camp, it was time for the
physical exam. I had been steadily increasing my push-up and sit-up
reps in the weeks prior to the final exam, so I felt fairly confident in
my ability to succeed in those. It was the two-mile run I was dread-
ing. I had passed the run before, but something about the oblong,
one-mile track we hadn't used before and the humidity of that South
Carolina morning was intimidating.

It was dawn, and I noticed the orange and purple hues blanketing
the sky in anticipation of sunrise. My entire company of sixty-plus
soldiers was at the track, ready to compete. I had a strategy for race
days: Start in the back, pace yourself, and kick it into high gear during
the final quarter mile. I saw no need to change that tactic this particular day. So after I stretched my already sore shins, I moseyed to the
back of the starting line.

Once the starting gun went off, the super soldiers took off running—they were the ones that excelled in every aspect of boot camp.
The other mere mortals at the back of the line and I were patiently waiting for the starting line crowd to thin out so we could proceed to jog.

Once I got up to the starting line, it was time to put my strategy to the test. I quickly moved over to the outside lane of the track, and after a few minutes, I settled into a steady eight-minute-mile pace. Before I knew it, I had completed one lap around the track and was halfway done.

The second lap was the worst. By this point, I was tired; I also was trying not to get sucked up by the faster runners and run out of gas before the end. As I rounded the last corner of the track onto the final straightaway, I could see the finish line ahead. *Almost there!* It was now time to take off.

I waited until I got to the last two hundred yards and then broke into a full sprint—my long legs stretched out almost parallel to the track. Like the Road Runner cartoon, I breezed by the wannabe super soldiers that failed to pace themselves earlier in the race and were now losing steam.

I finally crossed the finish line, passing the benchmark with a 15:47 time. With my forty-one push-ups and seventy-three sit-ups, I aced the overall fitness exam! When I finished my army reserve training that December, I had gained six pounds of muscle, could run for miles, and was in the best shape of my life.

Freshmen Fifteen

After returning from the army reserves, the daily workouts I had sustained for five months during training quickly dissipated. For the first month or so, I got up before 5:00 a.m. out of habit to jog around my neighborhood. But outside of the constant structure of reveille wake-ups and drill sergeants, it was hard to maintain that type of discipline. I slowly started to sink back into my old routines, which did not involve getting up before the sun.

I had delayed entering college by one semester to attend boot camp. When the spring semester came around that January, I was eager to get started. I had deferred my acceptance to San Diego State in the fall to join the army, but after being so far away from home in South Carolina, I wasn't ready to go to school eight hours away. I decided to attend Cal State University Sacramento instead, a two-hour drive from the Bay Area. This was the perfect distance for me to move out of my parents' house and establish life as an adult but still be close enough to come home if I needed to.

College life was a blur. What I do remember is that college was where I learned to put my body by the wayside. By my second semester, I was working twenty to thirty hours a week to pay for my off-campus studio apartment while maintaining a full course load. I had perfected my schedule and was taking classes all day on Tuesdays and Thursdays and then working the other days as an assistant manager at Rave, a discount clothing chain for teens.

When I wasn't studying or working, I was hanging out with my then-boyfriend, Al. He and I met at the end of my senior year in high school and had been maintaining a long-distance relationship while I was away in the army reserves. When I moved to Sacramento for school, Al remained in the Bay Area, working full-time. Every weekend, either he or I would drive down or drive up to see each other.

I was routinely burning the candle at both ends—working late at the mall, up early studying, and spending whatever little free time I had with Al. At nineteen, I think my body was primed to handle the lack of sleep, so I could easily function most days. What my body couldn't maintain was my army-sized weight. Margarita Mondays and Taco Tuesdays quickly led to the Freshmen Fifteen and beyond.

Weight was never an issue in my life until college. At first, I didn't think much of the extra pounds invading my midsection. It's easy to integrate twenty extra pounds into your reality with new clothes and a busy schedule that leaves no time to realize.

Looking back, it was during these years in college that I learned
to disassociate from my body on a recurring basis.

I learned to ignore my body's signals that I was becoming off bal-
ance. The fatigue and weight gain were easily overlooked in the name
of getting it all done. I had the single-minded focus of a toddler with a
tablet. It was school, study, work. Then rinse and repeat for four years
until graduation was in sight. There was no time to be in tune with
my body. I had big plans to complete. But once I became pregnant in
my final semester of college, there was no escaping my body and the
fact that it would never be the same.

Ready, Set, Go

Walking across the stage to receive my college diploma while four
months pregnant was not in my original plans. Al and I had gotten
married the year before and had talked about starting a family once I
got settled in my career. But this was one of those times when life had
other plans, and I had no choice but to embrace the fact that I was
about to bring a precious baby boy into the world. I was twenty-four
and experiencing so many things in my body for the first time, including rapid weight gain. By the time our son, Morgan, was born, I had
gained sixty pounds and was unrecognizable to myself.

After Morgan was born, I decided to quit my job to stay home
with him. I landed a role as an HR manager at Target when I graduated. But the rotating schedule of nights and weekends was not
conducive to caring for a newborn. Plus, I was tired of living in Sacramento and wanted to get back to the Bay Area and my family. This
would also provide me with better job prospects once I was ready to
return to the workforce, which I knew would be soon.

As much as I loved staying home with my son, on most days, I
felt like I was missing out on this grand career I had planned. I loved

being a mom, but I also wanted to work. I wasn't sure I was even cut out for motherhood because it was so foreign in the beginning. I was terrified of my ability to keep this precious little being alive, and I regularly checked to make sure he was still breathing in the middle of the night. I eventually got the hang of it, but it was hard feeling so inadequate in the most important job of my life.

What I knew for sure how to do was work. I knew how to work hard and accomplish any goal I set my mind to. That next goal turned out to be getting back to work and starting my ascent up the corporate ladder.

When Al and I were settled in the Bay Area, I quickly found a temp assignment working in HR for Mervyns. As I mentioned earlier, to this day, Mervyns is one of the best places I've worked and is where I got my first taste of leadership. I also experienced the buzz of a fast-paced career, which was intoxicating. I didn't mind commuting to work or traveling between sites on a special assignment if it meant advancing my career.

On most days, though, I struggled to get through all my meetings, calls, and emails so I could pick up Morgan from daycare by 6:00 p.m. Thank God the amazing daycare he attended was just fifteen minutes from my job. Once I picked him up, it was time to rush home and prepare dinner since Al had already gone to work on the swing shift as a machine operator at Berkeley Farms. After dinner, it was bath time and then bedtime stories before getting a moment of rest myself. I was floating on autopilot most days. The body kept score, and so far, I was still winning. Unbeknownst to me, I was in the first inning of a major league series, and my body was about to strike out.

Even though I was no longer in boot camp running miles, in those early years of my corporate career, my life felt like a racetrack, and I couldn't quite keep pace. And before I knew it, years had gone by in a flurry. For eight long years, my life ran at a pace that would make Usain Bolt envious.

During those years, Al and I were both working but barely making enough money to make ends meet. This constant feeling of financial insecurity made me even more determined to work myself to the brink to succeed. This resulted in volunteering for special assignments to set myself up for promotion and switching jobs every couple of years to keep climbing the ladder and increasing my pay.

I'm not sure if I put most of the pressure on myself with my relentless drive to succeed or if I was running from the circumstances I found myself in. Either way, my body had settled into a rhythm of relentless motion. That was, until I woke up one morning with chest pains, convinced I was having a heart attack.

A Body in Motion

Al rushed me to the emergency room that morning because my chest hurt so much that I was barely able to breathe. After hours of waiting and routine tests, they discovered I was severely anemic, and that was causing the chest pains, shortness of breath, and fatigue. I had known I had iron-deficiency anemia from a blood test that was done when I was in the army reserves. However, this diagnosis never bothered me other than feeling colder than normal. But this time, the level of iron in my blood and my iron reserves were so low that the doctor prescribed a month of rest and treatment to recover. I couldn't believe it. A month? How could I take a month off work during one of the busiest times in my career?

My month of forced rest occurred in 2013 when I was working as a regional human resources manager for Under Armour. In that role, I was responsible for advising store managers, district managers, and regional leaders on talent strategies such as hiring and development, along with coaching them on how to address employee performance issues and misconduct. I loved helping these leaders solve their people-related problems. I was excellent at it, and the role had the added perk of regular travel to the sixty stores that belonged to my region.

The downside, of course, was the long hours. Because the company was based in Baltimore, Maryland, I often started work early California time to respond to emails from corporate and then would work late into the evenings to jump on calls with managers or employees on the West Coast. I was so used to being always on and available that I didn't know how to tell my boss that I needed to take some time off. Luckily, my boss Alex was incredibly understanding and encouraged me to take the time I needed to recover.

It was obvious I needed the time off. My skin looked dull. My breathing was labored. I could have slept twenty-four hours a day and still would have been tired. I had a general malaise that signaled something in my body was off. Despite all this, I was reluctant to take time off because I had become so used to ignoring my body's signals and pushing through. My "Strong Black Woman" conditioning was my operating system, but I didn't have the level of awareness to recognize it. After some convincing from my husband, I reluctantly complied with the doctor's orders and took a leave of absence. After a month of rest and daily iron supplements, my fatigue was gone, and I was ready to conquer the world again. Or so I thought.

The Body Always Keeps Score

The physicist Sir Isaac Newton discovered that a body in motion stays in motion. That is until that body finally breaks down from being under constant duress. In 2016, I learned yet again that my body has its limits and that no amount of pushing past the gas warning light will make it run further without a pit stop to refuel.

At this point in my career, I was working in the tech industry.

Looking around the office, I was painfully aware that I was one of the estimated 3 percent of Black women working in the tech field[13]—a fact that motivated me to be exemplary to make it easier for Black women to follow me through those doors. I suppose it was that underlying script of "You've got to work twice as hard to prove them wrong" that landed me in the Worker's Comp clinic one fall afternoon.

I rushed into the clinic, nearly late for my appointment, because the meeting I had prior ran over. When I entered the brightly lit waiting room, I was visibly annoyed to see so many people waiting ahead of me. *Ping. Buzz. Ping.* My work notifications were going off like fireworks, which only exacerbated my anxiety at having to take time off work that afternoon to be seen. But I had no choice.

My right wrist was in constant pain when I typed, and that pain had begun to shoot up my forearm to my elbow. My arm was bristling from what felt like a thousand tiny needle pricks, and some days my pinky and ring fingers felt numb. I tried treating the pain myself with ibuprofen and taking the breaks recommended on the ubiquitous ergonomic flyers posted around the office. This only provided temporary relief. And readily responding to work emails, texts, and pings from sunup past sundown definitely wasn't helping.

As I sat there in the waiting room waiting for the medical assistant to call me for my appointment, I eagerly took out my work phone like a fiend to see what communication I'd missed on the ten-minute drive to the clinic. As I scrolled through emails, my right wrist throbbed with the rising pressure of a teakettle ready to boil. I was joined by a steady flow of men and women, many of whom were dressed in work uniforms. It suddenly dawned on me that I seemed to be the only one there who had hurt herself using a keyboard instead of a power tool.

---

13 Matthew Urwin, "Women in Tech Statistics: Despite Great Strides, Challenges Persist," Built In, April 13, 2023, https://builtin.com/women-tech/women-in-tech -workplace-statistics.

I finally made it into the exam room and was quickly joined by a nice, noticeably young male doctor who sat down on a rolling stool in front of my exam table to ask me some questions about why I was there. After hearing my laundry list of symptoms and the embarrassing amount of time I had waited to make the appointment, he recommended I go to physical therapy, take some medication for the nerve pain, and, most importantly, slow down on the volume of work to ease the repetitive stress I was putting on my wrist. He might as well have told me to jump off a building. *Slow down? Be serious, Doc!* I smiled and nodded and promised him I'd do better, then rushed back to work so I could make my afternoon meetings.

I continued at this "get it all done at any cost" pace until 2021, when the universe benched me again with my husband's death. In the initial weeks after Al's death, I was under constant siege from mental anguish, so it was easy to ignore my body aches and fatigue. But soon enough, I began to realize that I could barely make it through the day without a nap. And I wasn't napping to escape my grief. I was physically exhausted all the time.

No one had ever told me that grief is as much a physical journey as it is a mental and spiritual one. Some of the most common physical symptoms of grief include extreme fatigue, body aches, pain, digestive issues, brain fog, lowered immunity to infection, and an increased risk of heart disease.[14] Grief had overtaken my body, and this time I couldn't just ignore or simply work my way through it.

Signs of Life

During my bereavement leave, it was typical for me to stay up late, mindlessly bingeing on TV to take my mind off the hole in my heart. This meant that getting up with a cheery, rested disposition was out of

---

14 Ilene Raymond Rush, "What Are the Physical Symptoms of Grief?", Psycom, October 17, 2022, https://www.psycom.net/physical-symptoms-of-grief.

the question. On one particular morning, I woke up as usual feeling like a wreck, but a whisper in my spirit told me to get on the floor and stretch. Before I could talk myself out of the idea, I rolled out of bed and went in search of my yoga mat. Luckily, I had stashed one in my bedroom closet, so I didn't have to go downstairs to hunt for one in the garage.

I rolled out my mat next to my bed and quickly found a basic flow on YouTube to guide me. During the pandemic, I took up yoga to ease the stress of my job at Instagram. I had become very familiar with beginner yoga moves and flows but still preferred to follow along with someone more qualified. For the next fifteen minutes, I followed my virtual instructor intently, glancing up at the TV mounted on the wall to make sure I was getting each pose right. Before I knew it, my body had taken over and given my mind the break it desperately needed. Once the flow was over, I lay flat on my mat in the Savasana, or corpse pose, with sweat on my brow and endorphins kicking in, making me feel better than I had in months.

Just when I thought I could bask in that moment of physical relief forever, I heard Al's voice whisper from within, *I'm with you*. All of a sudden, I felt a warmth wash over my entire body, and I could feel his spirit engulfing me as I lay there, overcome with tears. I believe he was indeed with me, and that first yoga practice since he passed was the unexpected gift my body needed to get back in gear.

Trauma and stress affect the human body in profound ways. In his groundbreaking book, *The Body Keeps the Score*, Dr. Bessel Van Der Kolk explains that "trauma compromises the brain area that communicates the physical, embodied feelings of being alive."[15] After the trauma of losing Al so suddenly, I felt like I was orbiting above my body like a satellite. I felt out of sync. I was fractured in shards that I didn't know how to reconcile.

---

15 Bessel Van Der Kolk, MD, *The Body Keeps the Score: Brain, Mind, and Body in the Healing of Trauma* (New York: Penguin Publishing Group, 2014).

But doing just a few minutes of yoga made me feel connected to myself again. There is something about feeling your heartbeat that offers a subtle reminder that you exist. From that moment, I was determined to make movement a part of my daily routine.

At the beginning of my yoga quest, I settled for whatever quick routine the algorithm served up. Then one morning, I stumbled upon a quirky-looking guy with a topknot and a too-tight T-shirt who introduced me to what quickly became my lifeline, Kundalini yoga. Mr. Topknot had his own yoga channel dedicated to Kundalini yoga. On his channel, I came across his thirty-day Kundalini yoga challenge and decided to give it a try. *How bad could this be?* At the very least, I'd get a kick out of his goofy grin and overwhelming positivity.

I would later learn that Kundalini yoga is a combination of yoga traditions designed to raise complete body awareness through physical postures and breathwork. In Hinduism, Kundalini is a form of diving feminine energy believed to be at the base of the spine. For thirty days, I awkwardly contorted myself into bends and folds while learning the breath of fire and other breathwork techniques designed to activate different chakras.

Once I overcame the physical discomfort of learning those initial moves, I eased right into the practice. I began to look forward to my sessions and the peace I felt afterward. As I learned more about Kundalini, I understood why my spirit was drawn to it. I learned that Kundalini is a method for releasing trauma and grief in the body.

I continued my yoga practice once I returned to work. On days when I couldn't find thirty or more minutes to practice, I would stretch or meditate instead—those brief moments of movement each day helped me to come alive again. The sensation of feeling my blood pumping and my chest rising up and down vigorously with every challenging pose was like reconnecting with a long-lost love. I was in my body again. As Dr. Van Der Kolk discovered in his research, yoga is a "terrific way to (re)gain a relationship with the interior world and with it a caring, loving, sensual relationship to the self."

I was so thankful to have finally returned home to myself. And it didn't require me to become a triathlete or sign up for an expensive gym membership. Of course, if you're into intense exercise, you should fully embrace it! However, it doesn't require extreme sacrifice to reconnect to your body. I've found that consistency is the real key. Find something you can do consistently that makes your body feel alive.

By the time I returned to work in August 2021, I had established a consistent routine of movement and was feeling great. It was easy to fit in my morning yoga in the beginning because I wasn't working at full capacity. My manager and I met my first week back to work and agreed upon a transition plan that would ease me back gradually to a full workload. My inner beast mode had been dormant for months, so a part of me was eager to get back to full speed, even if it was just a distraction from my grief.

But a growing part of me had been through my own Armageddon and had come out the other side changed. I was exhausted from running at full speed my entire life and had gotten a taste of peace. In order to hold on to my peace, I would have to arm wrestle with some long-held beliefs about rest and my worth.

FIVE

Twice as Hard

"What would it be like to live a life of leisure every day?
Can't we always hit the pause button, though? Seems like
I'm always on fast-forward or rewind, though. No time to
stop the grind—or can I set the pace and still win the race?"
—MY JOURNAL, 3.11.22

I was born in East Palo Alto, California, or EPA for short. In the early 1980s, East Palo Alto was a predominantly Black community of about eighteen thousand residents, many of whom migrated to Northern California from the segregated South in the 1960s and '70s like my parents had. Through racially discriminatory housing practices preventing people of color from renting or buying homes in nearby Palo Alto, East Palo Alto was redlined into existence. It was a Black and Brown settlement cut off from the surrounding affluence of our White neighbors by a freeway and an overpass—the latter being the line of demarcation between two worlds you'd better be careful when crossing.

I knew this overpass from East Palo Alto and Palo Alto along University Avenue very well as a child. My mother would have to venture to Palo Alto to "do business," as she would say, which meant running errands such as going to the bank or post office. We would leave East Palo Alto in my mom's bluish-gray Ford Tempo, and in two left turns, we'd be on University Avenue. I used to look out the back seat window and study my surroundings the whole way.

In East Palo Alto, we passed modest homes with several cars out front belonging to the multiple family members living inside. We passed empty lots and bus stops with mothers waiting with small children and strollers in tow. We passed people hustling to get to work and school and people on the corner hustling whatever they could sell to get by.

As we crossed over the Highway 101 overpass into Palo Alto, one of the first things that greeted us was a new county and city line. As we drove past the border from San Mateo into Santa Clara County, trees lined the freshly swept streets, creating a canopy of bright green foliage that I loved to look up at as we drove underneath.

I was in awe of the perfectly manicured lawns and houses with stone columns and cars with funny names that I had never heard of before. In East Palo Alto, the weather felt cold most days, and the atmosphere seemed gray. But in Palo Alto, the sun always seemed to be smiling in the sky while showering us with her golden rays. It felt quite literally like a night-and-day difference. And, in fact, it was.

By the late 1980s, East Palo Alto had become another American city overrun by drugs—from a bustling community of Black love, pride, and hope to a powder keg of poverty, economic abandonment, and despair in the span of twenty years. Meanwhile, Palo Alto and the surrounding Silicon Valley were busy birthing new technology and amassing unlimited wealth.

The state of these two communities couldn't have been more

different in 1989. And as an eight-year-old child riding in the back of my mom's car, it was plain enough for me to see that Palo Alto was a better place to live and that it wasn't meant for people who looked like me.

As a little girl, I wondered why we couldn't have nice things like the people in Palo Alto. I observed the adults around me working so hard but still struggling to make ends meet. It was in this context that I began to see that the world and the rules were different for Black people. And before I could fully experience this world of difference, my parents had to make sure I understood that I would have to make up the difference with hard work.

Twice as Good

I don't recall the first time they said it, but throughout my childhood, my parents told me, "You have to work twice as hard for half as much." This saying is so common within the Black community that the sentiment showed up on the popular ABC show *Scandal* in a 2013 episode where the father of Kerry Washington's character, Olivia Pope, scolded her and told her that she had to be "twice as good as them to get half of what they have"—a reference to her navigating Washington, DC, politics as a Black woman.

Whether it was conveyed to me as "twice as hard" or "twice as good," the underlying message was still the same. I understood as a child that I would need to do more than my White counterparts to get ahead in this society. My parents instilled in me the importance of education starting in kindergarten. They knew from their lived experience that as a Black person, and even more so as a Black woman, my credentials would be questioned at every juncture. My parents prepared me for life the only way they knew how which was to equip me early on to be ready to compete on an uneven playing field.

These early lessons from my parents would prove beneficial many times throughout my life. Even though I knew to expect to have my work overlooked or discounted, it was still shocking the first time it happened in real life.

"Congratulations, Regina," my boss told me after calling me into her office to talk that Monday morning. She was technically my skip-level manager and the HR director for our department. I sat across from her desk in one of the two mahogany chairs that were part of the cookie-cutter furniture set all the company's executives had in their offices. I had gone in there with butterflies in my stomach because I had just started my job there as an HR representative a month ago and was worried she was going to tell me it wasn't working out.

Instead, she looked at me with a wide-mouthed grin and said, "We're going to increase your salary by three thousand dollars annually to put you in line with your peers." I sat in my chair and blinked a few times before automatically responding, "Thank you so much," with an artificial grin that masked my disbelief. Not knowing how else to respond, I looked like one of the animatronics from Disneyland's "It's a Small World" ride, blinking and nodding robotically.

As my director sat behind her desk, rambling on about how happy they were to have me on the team, I was quietly seething with rage. They were increasing my salary to be *in line* with my peers, meaning I was currently being paid less than them! I couldn't believe it! What made this revelation a particular slap in the face was the fact that my peers and I did *the exact same job*.

All five of us had been hired within a few weeks of each other as HR representatives. Since we started around the same time, we were treated as a cohort and completed all our onboarding activities together. As a result, we became fast friends. And as new work friends, we talked about one another's backgrounds and work histories. We even showed one another our resumes. That's how I knew I had as much or more work experience as them. I also had the most direct experience, having done this exact corporate HR representative job for two years at my previous employer. Despite my work history, education, and how well I thought I interviewed, apparently, they had decided to pay me three thousand dollars less when I was hired.

My director never gave me an explanation for this devastating discrepancy. As I've reflected on this over the years, I can only assume that unconscious bias was at play. I was the only Black woman hired on the HR representative team at the time. The White, Asian, and LatinX peers in my cohort mirrored the racial makeup of the company. One of our strongest tendencies as humans is to seek and identify with an in-group. And we tend to be more comfortable with and overly generous to members of our group, which is known as "similar to me" or affinity bias.

Whether it was an unconscious decision to discount my experience and pay me less or an overt bias, it didn't matter. Either way, I left my HR director's office that day feeling confused, angry, and absolutely determined to prove to them that they had grossly underestimated me.

There are some things you can't unknow. And knowing that you were perceived as less than your peers in some way, evidenced by the difference in salary, is unforgettable. This annoying fact became like an albatross, mentally weighing me down each day. It triggered a defensiveness in me to prove I was worthy.

Throughout my first year of working there, I found myself constantly comparing myself to my peers and trying to separate myself from the pack. In staff meetings, when one of the other HR representatives would speak up about how they had a difficult client group, which is how we referred to the internal departments we provided HR support to, I'd snicker to myself and think, *Huh, try having two difficult client groups to support.* Or I'd roll my eyes and think, *Aren't you supposed to have it harder since you supposedly have more experience?* Petty, I know. But the drama over my salary created a false sense of inferiority that was hard to shake.

I knew it wasn't my coworkers' fault. We all became good friends at work and even hung out outside of work. Some of us are still friends to this day. But that didn't stop me from secretly competing with them to show our bosses how good I knew I was. Soon enough, though, I would receive a new opportunity that would finally put the competition in my mind to rest.

The company, a national grocery store chain that carries thousands of name brands, also manufactures its own private-label products. In 2009, about a year into my tenure, the company hired a new senior vice president with a track record in consumer-packaged goods to revamp the strategy for the store's private brands. This new SVP needed dedicated HR support to help him and his leadership team restructure the company's Consumer Brands department, which turned out to be the opportunity I had been waiting for.

I had spoken to my HR director a few weeks prior, letting her know I was interested in a stretch assignment. I had succeeded in getting promoted at my former employer by volunteering for extra projects, so I made it a practice at this job to let everyone know I was seeking a challenge—my manager, my peers, the random person walking by my desk—okay, I'm kidding about that part. But I would enthusiastically tell anyone who I believed could help me that I was ready for more!

Because I had planted the seed earlier, my HR director circled back to me and asked if I'd be interested in a temporary assignment supporting Consumer Brands. She said I would be the dedicated HR partner for the new SVP and his team and would need to help them figure out their HR strategy. She wasn't sure about the exact scope of the assignment yet, but she thought it would last at least six months.

I eagerly jumped at the chance, nearly leaping out of my chair to say yes, I'd do it!

After some final negotiations with my manager on who would support my existing clients, I was assigned to the Consumer Brands team. The team was in a newer building at a different address, down the street from our main campus. The new building was chicer than the building I worked in. It had a sleek steel-and-glass design with massive windows and newer furniture to complement its more modern layout. I walked into the building the first time, feeling like I had made it to the Big Leagues.

It wasn't long before I realized I was out of my league, at least in the beginning. I was able to introduce myself to Joe, the senior vice president of the department. He seemed nice enough, but I could tell he was on a serious mission to implement significant changes, and I would need to bring my A game to support him. The problem was that I didn't really know how to play the game at this level. Sure, I had supported other senior leaders before, but those had been established teams. I didn't have any experience helping a team develop a people plan to support a new business strategy and team structure. I was so green and, in some ways, still finding my voice that I hesitated to speak up and ask the right questions in the beginning or assert myself in the right meetings. This led to an early setback that nearly cost me the assignment.

I was a few weeks into my temp role and had gotten wind that Joe wanted to have a discussion about reorganizing his team. A change like that could impact people's jobs, so it was crucial to have HR and legal counsel at the onset. However, I failed to flag this meeting for my boss in advance, and I hadn't asked to be invited to the meeting myself to ensure someone from HR was present. Somehow our VP of HR got wind of it and decided to attend. It was good that he was there to provide guidance, but he was none-too-pleased to be surprised by it.

Later that day, I was coached by my HR director that I should have been aware of that meeting and should have attended. She had a point. As the HR representative for this team, I was responsible for guiding the leaders on the major decisions impacting people, which required me to be in the room when decisions were being made. I'm not sure what stung more, her displeasure with me or my own disappointment at the reality that she was right. I let my fear of saying the wrong thing keep me on the sidelines of the biggest game of my career.

Ouch. I felt like I had dropped the ball and let my leadership team down. But this miss on my part ultimately showed me that I couldn't afford to be shy or play small. I would need to assert myself and push into the rooms I needed to be in to provide the HR guidance required to deliver the business results Joe had committed to.

From that point on, I went from quietly observing to pulling up to every meeting like I was VIP. I buttered up Joe's executive assistant to get regular time on his calendar and proceeded to do the same with the other admins so I could build relationships with Joe's staff. I realized I would have to earn their trust to be effective in my role. And there was no better way than to roll up my sleeves and get in the trenches with them to help each of them figure out how to structure their team in the wake of changes being brought on by Joe.

Once I got into the groove of things and began making relationships and being sought after for my advice, the work felt exhilarating. I became a trusted advisor to Joe and his leadership team, and together we redesigned the department's structure, created and filled around forty new positions, and came up with new organizational values to support a high-performance team culture. I was having the time of my professional life—so much so that I practically ignored the fact that I was working ten-to-twelve-hour days and becoming exhausted.

The work was so consuming that I had a hard time turning it off. I would rush to leave the office by 5:00 or 5:30 p.m. to pick up my son from daycare, trying desperately to get there by 6:00 p.m. to avoid the late fee and the working mom walk of shame. Because Al was working a swing shift, it was just Morgan and me at home in the evenings. Once we made it home, it was dinner time, bath time, and then my second work shift. I would be on my laptop until 10:00 or 11:00 p.m. some nights, answering emails and preparing files for the next day. Being on such a prestigious assignment was an honor. It also made me feel like I was constantly on display and that my work product had better be ready for examination, especially as the only Black person working with that leadership team.

After the six-month assignment was finished, my HR leadership team couldn't have been more pleased. I had represented them well. And Joe was so satisfied with my work that he decided to create a new HR manager role on his team for me, reporting directly to him. When he showed me his new org chart with the box that had my name in it, I was giddy inside, as though I'd won a career lottery.

Unfortunately, my bubble soon burst. No sooner had I scoped out an office next to Joe's to move into, my HR director denied his request. She said she couldn't have HR people reporting to other teams outside of HR, and she didn't have the head count to assign me to him permanently.

My director's decision made sense. Nonetheless, I was crushed. The air in my balloon was not only deflated but my hopes for a promotion were stomped on and set ablaze. I ended up being assigned back to my original client groups and was given a bump to senior HR representative. It wasn't the HR manager title I desperately wanted and had proven I was capable of after six months on center stage.

Similar to my last job, I had worked my ass off to prove how good I was, but this time it didn't pan out the way I expected. It wasn't all for nothing, though. The assignment accelerated my skills by two levels in a short period of time and boosted my confidence in myself exponentially. A more subtle change happened in my psyche.

This experience solidified the story I had been told all my life. You must work twice as hard or be twice as good . . . for half as much.

Rise and Grind

After leaving that company, my career went into hyperdrive. I took my lessons of self-confidence and determination and other, more negative learned behaviors like self-sacrifice and extreme work ethic and used that toxic blend of fuel to power my ascent up the corporate ladder.

After a series of calculated career jumps from the retail sector to the airline industry and then banking, I landed myself in my dream industry: technology. I completed my master's degree in Organization Development when I was working for Virgin America airlines. I loved Organization Development (OD) as a discipline. This is a niche area of HR that focuses on the health and effectiveness of organizations and helping org leaders successfully manage large-scale change. I was fascinated by all the theories of industrial psychology and human nature and couldn't wait to put those theories into practice.

I took a role at a regional bank to get some of this hands-on experience. Then an opportunity of a lifetime came up to work at one of the founding titans of Silicon Valley, Intel Corporation. I was so excited when one of the hiring managers reached out to me via LinkedIn to ask if I'd be interested in applying for an Organizational Effectiveness Consultant role at Intel. After a few rounds of interviews, including one that involved presenting my response to an OD case study they provided me, I was hired! If my special assignment at my last company was the Big Leagues, working at Intel was the World Series.

The career experiences leading up to this job, where I learned to work myself to exhaustion to prove my worth, were so ingrained at this point that they had become my basic operating system. My persistent drive and near obsession with securing my seat at the table was like one of those annoying background apps on your cell phone that you forget is open yet is steadily draining your battery life. From day one of stepping into Intel's impressive headquarters, I was on a mission to excel despite having a crippling fear that I wasn't good enough to work with some of the smartest engineers in the world.

"Don't psych yourself out," said one of my early mentors at Intel. I had confided in Val that I was intimidated by how smart everyone who worked there was.

"Keep in mind they're really smart in one thing, and you bring a whole set of skills they don't have, which is why they need your guidance."

Although there was some sarcastic humor in her comment, my mentor was right. She helped me to remember the range of talents I brought to the table. While I didn't know any coding languages and would never understand how to fabricate a microchip, I was a badass in HR and OD, and that revived confidence set me up for success.

I was now in a corporate fraternity of sorts with some of the brightest minds in Silicon Valley, and I was successfully holding my own. There, HR was seen as a partner to the business, and my unit of Org Effectiveness practitioners was called upon to advise on org design, team effectiveness, integration plans for new leaders, and so much more.

For the first time as an HR professional, I truly felt seen, heard, and respected for my expertise. And I loved my work colleagues. On the fourth floor where I sat, we were a motley crew of quirky people working in different parts of HR, but we formed a bond that still lasts to this day.

Looking back, Intel was a pivotal moment in my career—and it was also where I perfected working with sustained exhaustion. Before I started working there, Al and I had bought a house in

Brentwood, a lovely, affordable suburb in the East Bay Area surrounded by agriculture. We moved there because it is a nice, quiet community in which to raise a family. However, it's located nearly fifty miles from Intel's corporate headquarters in Santa Clara, which in Bay Area traffic translated to a two-hour commute to and from work most days.

I started my workdays exhausted from the commute alone. I would wake up at 5:00 a.m. and would have to leave the house by 6:00 a.m. to make the train on time or get ahead of the traffic if I was driving that day. And my stress level only went up from there. Toward the end of my time at Intel, one of the business units I was supporting was going through a high-stakes divestiture that required a delicate strategy to secure valuable engineering talent before the contentious relationship with the partner company imploded. Everything about this project was highly confidential, highly visible, and highly stressful.

During one particularly stressful week, I was asked to find emergency office space in case the partner company decided to lock our employees out of the building we shared during the difficult negotiations underway. Another day, I had to fly to and from Boise, Idaho, the same day to support one of the senior leaders in delivering the news to employees that we were ending the joint venture and whose roles would be impacted.

I would leave high-stakes negotiations in the office and step into difficulties at home, where my husband was battling bouts of depression that made it hard for him to function some days. As Al withdrew into himself to face his own demons, I overcompensated by trying to carry the load for him and be all things to and for everybody else.

I would arrive home around 6:30 or 7:00 p.m. wiped out but not able to fully relax because I had to make dinner, help Morgan with homework, or deal with dirty dishes. After hurriedly ticking those added duties off my to-do list for the night, I'd head upstairs to bed alone, feeling emotionally numb—yet my body was still revving from being in fifth gear all day.

Around this time, a friend of mine reached out about an implausible opportunity to lead a global function at her new employer.

"Gina, you should apply," Sharawn said, trying to convince me as I was perusing the aisles at Famous Footwear, looking for a pair of sneakers for Morgan. "They're looking for someone with a strong HR background who knows talent management. You would be perfect, and we'd get to work together again!"

Sharawn could sell water to a whale. By then, we'd known each other for nearly ten years, and I'd seen her powers of persuasion and general badassery in action from our days working together in the corporate office of that national grocery chain.

Most recently, I'd watched from afar as she advanced to vice president of Total Rewards at her new organization. Although she was right that I ticked off many of the boxes in the job specification, there was one glaring gap. I was an HR manager at Intel. This was a senior director role, and I didn't think there was a snowball's chance in Hades they'd entertain me for the position.

Luckily, I was wrong. In the summer of 2018, I was hired as the global head of Talent Management and Talent Development. I had no time to waste. I had to quickly get into character as I was cast in the biggest part of my career to play the leading lady, despite feeling like an understudy.

You know, in the movies, when things are going too well, and they switch up the music, and you realize something bad is about to occur? This is that point in my story.

Just when I thought I had overcome some massive hurdles and insecurities at the beginning of my new role at Flex, a family illness would send me spiraling deeper into grind mode to cope with the weight of it all.

Suffering in Silence

When my father finally worked up the courage to tell us he was diagnosed with throat cancer, it didn't seem real. Even though I knew he hadn't been feeling like himself and had discovered a strange bump on his neck, I was in denial. My father was the strongest person I knew. The thought of losing him was too painful to imagine or utter out loud.

Perhaps it was this form of active denial that prevented me from telling the members of my team what my family and I were going through. I led a function with nearly forty people reporting to me, and none of them knew I was saddled with the weight of the department, plus unpronounced grief as I watched my father and mother deal with his illness. Eventually, I found the courage to tell my manager Hans, and I confided in Sharawn. For a time, they were the only two I trusted with my dad's diagnosis. I was too afraid to let anyone else know I was having personal troubles for fear they would hold that against me.

It may sound odd for me to withhold something so obviously consuming. But when you're on a tightrope in the middle of the circus, one false move could prove deadly. Or at least it felt that way. I was just six months into my role, and while I had some quick, early wins, I still felt I was pushing a boulder uphill in the hopes that I'd get to the top and suddenly belong. I was putting enormous pressure on myself to deliver the right answers in meetings, make the right decisions on the budget, and keep a firm hand on the team in order to drive projects to completion on schedule. Meanwhile, my father was undergoing chemotherapy and disappearing before my eyes.

"Daddy, do you want the remote?" I asked as he was getting settled underneath the blanket the nurse had just handed him. I had decided to take my dad to his weekly chemo treatment. He was now a regular at the oncology clinic, and the staff there loved him. When we checked in twenty minutes prior, I had the chance to see his Southern charm on full display. He still had a way of making others smile, even when you could see he was in pain. After they checked him in, he found his favorite chair, and I sat right next to him, trying to be attentive but not awkwardly in the way.

"You can have the remote, Gene. Turn on whatever you want." Everyone in my family calls me Gina, but Daddy has always called me Gene for short. I was fiddling around with the remote like it was a foreign object as I tried to get comfortable in my reclining chair and forget that my dad was undergoing treatment to save his life. As Daddy sat back underneath his cozy blanket, dozing off to whatever was on the screen above us, it almost felt like he was at home in the living room—minus the tubes wrapping every which way around him.

"You sure you're comfortable, Daddy?" I asked. "Do you want me to get you something to drink?"

When he said yes, I went to find a nurse who could get him some juice. I learned there was a mini fridge in the clinic hallway where patients could help themselves to drinks and snacks. When I brought back his juice and a few snacks for us, Daddy told me, "It's okay if you get on the computer. I know you have work to do." Until that point, I had succeeded in not getting on my laptop, even though the stress of never-ending deadlines was eating away at me.

"Thanks, Daddy," I said sheepishly. I looked around the treatment room; I was the only one there with a laptop. A deep sense of shame washed over me as I clicked away on my keyboard, answering what amounted to meaningless emails in the face of cancer. Yet I couldn't help myself. *I know I need to be here for Daddy*, I thought. *But what if I drop the ball?*

It seems absurd thinking about it now. What project, email, or decision couldn't wait eight hours for me to be fully and unequivocally present for my dad? There was none. The fear of being seen as incompetent or weak for being unable to juggle it all was all in my head.

But this mindset of working "twice as hard" was too engrained in me, despite the diminishing returns. I carried this pattern with me until my belief system was rebooted by Al's death.

New Boundaries

"How are you doing?" my colleague asked me. This would be a recurring question during my first days and weeks back to work at Instagram after Al passed. Although we were still working remotely and conducting meetings on Zoom, the sincere care and concern of my teammates were deeply felt across the screen.

It was August 2021, and my first week back felt surreal. I had been mentally preparing for weeks to return to work, but once the day came, I couldn't help but question what I was even doing there. My world had disintegrated just three months prior, and here I was on Zoom, pretending to care about diversity and inclusion. The truth was that I cared about nothing at that point in time. I was caught in the shadows like I had ventured to the Upside Down from Netflix's *Stranger Things* and was now watching a parallel version of my life.

Fortunately, I had an amazing manager who insisted I take things slow when I returned. Maryann was one of those rare managers who was a genuinely compassionate person inside and outside of the office. I remember being shocked to see her at Al's funeral but equally grateful she was there to show support. Once she and I aligned on what I should focus on during my first month back, I was off to the races, or so I planned.

Before my bereavement leave, there wasn't a problem I wouldn't tackle to achieve our goals of greater diversity, equity, and inclusion at Instagram. If I wasn't in meetings to raise awareness about our DEI strategy, I was influencing people behind the scenes to make fairer decisions that could benefit everyone—especially those who were underrepresented. In my mind, I was like a DEI superhero, on call to save the unconsciously biased from themselves.

But when I returned, I was a superhero without a cape or a cause. I was unmasked as a mere mortal who desperately wished for superpowers to bring her husband back to life. I made it through most meetings on autopilot while my mind drifted away from the present to the life I had lost. In the early months of my grief, drifting away was a useful coping mechanism. Just as you can't stare at the sun, you can't stare at pain too long before turning away.

It wasn't long, though, before my apathy and avoidance shape-shifted into a more helpful state of mind—a new perspective. I had just lost my partner of twenty-one years, but instead of retreating from life and myself, I hung on and wrestled my anxiety and anguish to the ground so I could finally breathe again. So I could live again.

And I now understand how precious and fleeting life is. Through Al's death, I got a peek behind the curtain of a vast universe where loved ones move on but are always present and connected to us in spirit. I felt like I had an invisible scar and now belonged to an otherworldly sorority of people who have been touched by death and now see life more clearly.

You see, from that spiritual vantage point, how could life's trivial worries get me down? It became so easy for me to know where the boundary lines were between work, my personal life, and me. In the past, I was so invested in my career that I mistook it for who I was. For a time, work was all I felt I was any good at. But Al's death stripped away any false notions of who I was or was pretending to be. It left me bare in front of the mirror to clearly see myself. And I was beginning to love the new me.

At first, I felt guilty for saying no to certain things. But then my new perspective would kick in, and I'd know I was doing the right thing.

"Would you like to attend this meeting?" they asked.

No, thanks. I don't think it's necessary at this stage for me to attend.

"Do you want to be copied on the email?"

Nope. I see my team member is already included.

"Can we meet at 8:00 a.m. tomorrow?"

I'm not available at that time, but I'll ask my assistant to find us a time that works for both of us.

I became a boundary ninja, slicing through unreasonable requests for my time on a daily basis. And it felt so good!

It's true that death changes you. In my case, Al's death gave me mental freedom I hadn't experienced since childhood. My entire adult life, I had been told or had been telling myself stories about who I needed to be and how I needed to behave in the world to get ahead. But those beliefs kept me running on a track solo, competing against the enemies in my mind.

Before this awakening, I would panic if I forgot to send an email at 10:00 p.m., knowing full well the person on the other end wouldn't see it until the morning. I'd stress about saying the right thing in meetings or delivering the perfect presentation in front of a group of leaders. For my entire career, I was obsessed with proving them wrong and working twice as hard to get ahead. My single-minded focus on what I thought was success led me to miss out on dinners with my family, drinks with friends, and truly being present for my dad when he faced his life-and-death struggle.

All of that now paled in comparison to me making sure I was healthy and whole. Nowadays, I still work hard to achieve my goals, but I'm clear on which are really worth striving for and which are the ghosts of my ego's past. I have become an expert at discerning what truly needs my attention versus what I can defer, delegate, or delete (which I refer to as my "3D Time Ownership" framework).

Of course, this change in mindset hasn't been seamless. At times, I still find myself having thoughts of insecurity or feeling triggered to outperform. The difference now is that I can recognize this inner gremlin, and once I'm aware of these negative thoughts, I can choose differently. From awareness comes choice. And now that I've integrated myself fully back into life, I choose to live it unbound.

SIX

Resuscitation

*"Don't you want to breathe again? Don't you want
to feel again? Don't you want to just BE again . . .
be anything . . . be vibrant and alive?"*

—MY JOURNAL, 12.9.21

had made it to fall 2021, and after being back to work for two months and experiencing some semblance of normalcy, I still felt like a freak of nature with a deceased husband.

In many ways, Al's death felt like an accident by God or an outlier on the universe's timeline. Suddenly, I felt distinct from everyone I knew and everything I had known. Having lost my spouse at the age of forty made me different from my peers and the older widows sending me their condolences.

My life just felt different. I was now different. It felt strange for me to navigate the world on my own after having shared twenty-one years with my other half.

On the outside, I was functioning well. I would wake up when I was supposed to, walk the dog, eat breakfast, get dressed, and usually get on Zoom by 8:30 a.m. each morning to begin my workday. I'd attend meeting after meeting, contributing my thoughts with the requisite smile to show everyone I was "okay." On the inside, however, I was muddling through my grief each day, feeling suffocated by the weight of it all.

I had been in individual therapy for my grief since Al died in May. Since then, I had tried a couple of different grief groups, seeking comfort from others who could relate to my loss. But each group I tried made me feel more alone. And it wasn't the group's fault. Each consortium of grievers I encountered was perfectly nice to me when I signed on, yet I felt like an outcast due to the group structure or the circumstances of each member's bereavement.

One group consisted of people who had lost a loved one, not necessarily their spouse. I found this group by searching online for grief support in my area. When I joined the Zoom call, there were about twenty of us. The group's moderator welcomed us into the meeting with a warm and comforting tone, reminiscent of my son's kindergarten teacher, who used to greet each student entering her class with a hug. As the Zoom squares began to populate the screen, I could see a mixture of women and men, most of whom appeared older than me.

The grief group was scheduled for one hour, and anyone could sign up to join the ongoing sessions. Each session was structured to be relatively free-flowing. Our moderator would start by reminding us of the rules to listen respectfully and then would turn it over to someone to share about their loss. We would then go around the virtual room, with each person taking two to three minutes to share whatever was top of mind for them relative to their grief.

I was too nervous about being the first to share, so I sat quietly on mute listening to each person reopen their wound and reveal their brokenness. By the time it came around to me, I had decided that I would be brief and not bare the depths of my soul. Perhaps I just wasn't comfortable with the group yet. This was my first day attending, after all. And after listening to several stories, it was clear to me that the unexpected nature of my loss and the aftermath of my life was different. It wasn't that my pain was any worse than theirs; it was just that I was seeking an example of another young widow to relate to because their life shattered in its prime with a kid still at home to raise.

After the session was over, I was emotionally drained. The empath in me had absorbed the group's agony for over an hour and added their emotions to my own warehouse. I felt more depressed than before the call started. After trying the group one more time, I decided I couldn't bear the pain of the open-share format and began looking for other ways to express my grief to others.

I had mentioned to my primary therapist that I wanted to find a grief group to join. Lucky for me, she had a few referrals, including one for a grief writing group. *Writing could be good for me*, I thought. Since I was a little girl, I have always kept a journal, and in the weeks and months since Al died, I had written notes nearly every day to process my pain. My therapist thought this particular grief group would benefit me because the therapist who ran it kept the groups small, and each group was focused on a different type of loss—for instance, people who've lost their spouse or parents who have lost a child.

The next day, I reached out to Joan, the organizer of the grief writing group. Joan told me she was a licensed therapist and grief counselor and had been running her Writing Through Grief Workshop alongside her private practice for many years. To my delight, she was in the process of forming an online group for younger widows. I was thrilled at the possibility of finding women in a similar situation as me to commiserate with.

I was excited at the possibility of this grief group becoming an emotional lifeline for me in ways that family and friends couldn't relate to. What I wasn't prepared for was the process and how it would expose the next layer of emotions I needed to heal.

Ripping Off the Band-Aid

Remember the roller coaster of emotions you felt as a kid when you fell off your bike or did something else to earn yourself a scrape worthy of a Band-Aid? I remember falling off my bike and skinning my knee more than once as a child.

At first, I felt the rush of pain as my knee hit the gravel, followed by the burn of peroxide once my mom began to patch me up with her first aid kit. Then, after we both blew on it, I felt the cool relief of the Neosporin and a Band-Aid to protect the wound so it could begin to heal.

In some ways, grief was like skinning my knee. After the initial pain and shock, I covered up the wound after the funeral with pleasantries and a return to daily life in an attempt to heal. But just like wearing a Band-Aid, at some point, you need to rip that thing off and expose your wound to the air so it can finally scab over and fully heal.

I had been dealing with my grief on a surface level up to that point, only allowing myself to know the depths of my heartache. It was finally time to excavate my sorrow and bring my pain to the light. I decided to join the Young Widows Grief Writing Workshop and braced myself for the necessary healing that only spilling my emotional guts could bring.

Our group's first virtual meeting was on November 8, 2021. Five of us shell-shocked widows assembled on Zoom, and Joan quickly introduced herself and explained how each session would work. We would start with a short poem or writing excerpt and then be given about twenty minutes to write how we felt about the writing, followed by each person sharing what they had written with the group

Before Joan gave us the writing prompt, she asked each of us to introduce ourselves. It was awkward enough to meet for the first time online. Add the fact that each of us had lost our spouse within the last year, and you could cut the anxiety with a knife. Thankfully Joan had run these groups for a while and did a wonderful job holding space, including silence, for us to begin to open up.

The introductions were as painful an ordeal as you would expect. All five of us widows were in our forties, and each of us had kids. In comparison, I felt lucky only having one child who was now a teenager versus the other women struggling to piece together their lives while also caring for one or more children under the age of twelve.

Even though my situation was slightly different, for the first time since Al died, I felt truly seen and understood. Some of the women had a spouse die from illness, having to experience the added pain of watching their husband suffer for months before passing away. A couple of the women were like me, having their significant other stolen in an instant.

After our round of introductions, it was time to complete the writing prompt. The assignment was deceivingly simple. Joan asked us to free write for twenty minutes, using the phrase "This grief is . . ." followed by a description of our feelings. I grabbed my purple-and-gold embossed journal and proceeded to bare my soul. *Oh boy, here goes nothing . . .*

This grief is debilitating.

This grief is insidious. It seeps into every thought, every move, and every breath in my lungs.

This grief is selfish. It won't allow me to take my mind off it and comes back with a vengeance at the slightest hint of joy.

This grief is sad. More sad than I've ever felt in my life, and

I'm scared to feel this way for the rest of my life, but I'm terrified to let it go.

This grief is lonely. I don't know how to connect with others sometimes because they don't understand the magnitude of my loss.

This grief is haunting. It fills my nights with thoughts of him. With longing and regrets and desires to wind back time to have our love all over again.

This grief is awful. It sucks the life out of you and makes you wish you were dead.

This grief is a part of me. Like a scar I'll never get rid of or a wound that won't fully heal.

This grief is surprising in its depth and complexity, and magnitude. It swallows anyone and anything in its path.

This grief is special because it's shaped by the love I had for him. That's why I cling to the grief some days in remembrance of him.

This grief is necessary to honor my pain and my experience. I need this grief if I ever hope to deal with the terrible thing that happened to me and my son.

This grief is confusing. Some days I can talk about Al and laugh, and other times if I catch a glimpse of his picture out of the corner of my eye, I'm enveloped in tears.

This grief is strange that way. No rhyme or reason. No predictable pattern or warning. It's just raw, primal emotion of a love lost and a heart broken in two.

What comes of this grief? I hear it wanes over time, but at this stage, I'm skeptical if it'll ever go away.

I looked up from my journal after reading my piece to the group and was instantly comforted by the all-knowing eyes of other women who also had been thrust into the rotten club of widowhood.

For the next twelve weeks, I showed up to our grief writing group faithfully. Some days I dreaded attending because I knew during the session the pain of my own loss and the loss of the other women in the group was inescapable. The fact that my grief was inescapable in these meetings was the unexpected gateway to my healing.

Me, Myself, and I

Joining the Grief Writing Workshop was a lifeline in an ocean of despondency that had become my life. I was not only disconnected from life but from my own identity. I didn't recognize who I was anymore or who I wanted to be now that I was without my partner. Left to my own devices, I would have probably floated adrift for years had I not found a spiritual buoy—podcasts—to bring me back to shore.

I am a huge fan of podcasts. My love of podcasts started when I had my long commute to work. Listening to something educational or entertaining was a way to break up the monotony of hours on the road. During the pandemic, I no longer had a long commute, so I fell out of the habit of listening to podcasts. But during my bereavement leave, I suddenly had hours of time on my hands, and podcasts once again became a way to fill it.

During the summer I was off for bereavement, I stumbled upon Devi Brown's podcast *Dropping Gems*. Devi is a well-known radio personality who now serves others as a wellness educator and healer. Listening to the first episode of her podcast was like the precious first breath of air after being submerged underwater.

After a few episodes, I began to look forward to Devi's uplifting and inviting vibe and otherworldly wisdom. She was clearly a woman who had been through some hard things and had the spiritual scars to prove it. Devi seemed like a worthy guide as I was exploring who I was at this point in my life and what cosmic lesson Al's death was meant to send me.

On one summer morning in July, an episode of *Dropping Gems* caught my eye that I hadn't listened to yet. It was called "You Are Uniquely Designed with Erin Claire Jones."[16] Something about that title stirred in my spirit. *You are uniquely designed. For what?* I thought. *Hopefully not to be a sad and lonely widow for the rest of my life. Sheesh!* Even my self-talk was cynical.

I proceeded to listen to the episode in the background while I straightened up around the house. Devi opened the episode by describing how much she loves to deepen her learning of herself. *Ooh, a kindred spirit!* Devi's enthusiasm for soul searching caught my attention, especially since I was struggling to feel grounded in my new reality.

After a brief rundown of the theme of this episode, Devi introduced a tool for self-discovery I had never heard of before called Human Design. Devi described Human Design as a "synthesis of ancient wisdom and modern science that sheds light on a person's energetic makeup as well as specific tools that they can use to live at their happiest, healthiest, highest potential." My ears immediately perked up. I was desperate for anything that could spark happiness again. And I needed answers about whom I was meant to become because my life had taken a sharp detour from what I had planned.

Devi then introduced her guest, Erin Claire Jones, who is a renowned Human Design guide and leadership coach. Less than five minutes into their discussion, Erin hooked me with her point of view on the power of Human Design. "Human Design, more than anything else, just gives us permission to be ourselves." The phrase *permission to be ourselves* was like a lightning bolt directed to my soul.

Throughout so much of my life, I had to be someone else—someone quieter, someone stoic, someone compliant, someone

16 "You Are Uniquely Designed with Erin Claire Jones," *Deeply Well* podcast with Devi Brown, https://podcasts.apple.com/us/podcast/you-are-uniquely-designed-with-erin-claire-jones/id1458578448?i=1000529000240.

contained—to climb the corporate ladder to success. And that didn't include all the other "someones" I had to be as a wife, mother, daughter, sister, churchgoer, neighbor, and friend. I had spent my whole life trying to be everything to everybody and losing myself in the midst of it all.

However, once I began to dive into my Human Design, which is reflected in a body graph based on your birth date, birth location, and birth time, I instantly felt whole. Seeing my innate strengths and the revelation of how those combine to support my unique purpose was like finding the decoder ring for a buried treasure map. All this time, I had been striving to be more, do more, and have more when all I really needed to do was simply be myself and allow the universe to support my endeavors.

Through Human Design, I came to remember that I was never broken or unworthy. As Devi explained in that episode, often, we are conditioned to believe that there is something wrong with us. But in reality, "perhaps we are working with the wrong set of instructions," she explained. For the rest of that year, I devoured everything I could find about Human Design to understand better my personal set of instructions for living more fully.

The more I uncovered in my design, the more I wanted practical tools and guidance to put what I was learning into practice. I remembered how much Erin Claire Jones resonated with me as a Human Design coach because of her pragmatic approach. I decided to purchase a Human Design Blueprint from her company. The blueprint that arrived via email was roughly sixty pages long and gave a detailed breakdown of my chart, along with insights on how I use my energy best, how I make decisions, and how I express my identity, among other things.

I am a tactile reader who prefers to touch and feel the pages of anything I read, so I had my PDF version printed in color and bound. When I opened the beautiful, glossy booklet for the first time, I was immediately drawn to a few of the bolded statements on the first page:

YOU ARE DESIGNED TO BE A LEADER, VISIONARY, AND GUIDE,
TO FIND WHOLENESS THROUGH CONNECTION WITH OTHERS,
TO HONOR THE EBBS AND FLOWS OF YOUR ENERGY,
AND TO SLOW DOWN AND NOT APPLY A SENSE OF URGENCY TO EVERYTHING YOU DO.

The entire page was filled with direct statements like this, describing my unique design in empowering and actionable terms. That first page was so impactful that I began flipping through the rest of the pages like I was a kid scouring the Toys "R" Us catalog to make my Christmas list. After just a few minutes of exploration, I began to cry, realizing I had never felt so deeply understood and celebrated for who I am as I did reading this guide.

Understanding my design instantly made me want to live more in alignment with it and follow my instincts and desires to expand, live more fully, and connect with others. By the time I purchased this guide in October 2021, I had spent much of the previous four months in isolation and grief. It was now clear that it was time to come out of my protective shell and reconvene with the world.

Thank You for Being a Friend

With 2021 nearing its end, I was emotionally ready to reconnect with others beyond my immediate family. Spending time with the people I love has always brought me joy. That's why the statement "You are designed to find wholeness through connection with others" from my Human Design Blueprint resonated so profoundly with me. Throughout my life, I have always been a relationship builder and connector of people.

In middle school, I discovered the power of having a girl squad. When we moved from predominantly Black East Palo Alto to predominantly White Livermore, where I was one of only a few Black girls in my sixth-grade class, it was my girls and guy friends who gave me a sense of belonging.

On the first day of sixth grade, I met my lifelong best friend, Donisha. She was one of the handfuls of Black girls at Junction Elementary School that I clung to like wrinkles to linen. Our moms worked together at the VA Hospital, and from the time they conspired to introduce us that first morning of sixth grade, we were inseparable. You hardly ever saw one of us without the other.

While I could be reserved at times, quietly observing the scene to decipher how to fit in, Donisha was brazen in her unapologetic expression of being comfortable in her own skin. She had laser-sharp wit that still makes me laugh to this day. We would sit in her room for hours gossiping about which boy we liked while listening to music. She was the first to stretch my musical tastes by introducing me to artists such as Alanis Morissette and Jamiroquai.

At her house, I could also listen to CDs my parents didn't allow me to, like Snoop's 1993 debut *Doggystyle* and Outkast's *Southernplayalisticadillacmuzik*. Donisha was simultaneously a breath of fresh air and a third rail in my structured and predictable life in the suburbs. She was my encyclopedia of all things cool, my partner in middle school crime, and my Cyrano when I needed a slick line to say to a crush. More than anything, she was my sister, and we could and would tell each other anything. She always seemed to have the right answer for whatever problem plagued my day.

True to form, she reached out to me after Al died to offer some sweet comfort. We reminisced for hours about Al, me, her husband, Chris, and her hanging out over the years. Donisha, her husband, Chris, and Al all served in the navy, which made for some fun stories when we got together, including trash-talking about me, the only army vet of the group. That afternoon, shortly after Al died, she helped to remind me of the tenderness of Al's and my love story, providing a momentary lapse from the weight of what I had lost.

Over the years, I had lost touch with so many of my friends, some because I had moved away for college, while other ties just naturally loosened when we couldn't find the time to reach out to one another in the throes of life. One such friend who thankfully reappeared when I needed to be brought back to life was my high school homegirl Mariko.

Mariko and I met in the ninth grade when she sat behind me in social studies class. The class was arranged in four or five rows of desks instead of pods of four, presumably so we could pay better attention to the teacher. But that didn't stop us from passing notes and whispering while the teacher wasn't looking, which is precisely how my relationship with Mariko started.

I had just gotten settled in my chair and was trying to mentally prepare for another boring lecture when I felt a tap on my shoulder. "You're dating Alvin?" the girl sitting behind me said in the form of an accusatory question. I had obviously seen her in class, but we had never spoken before that moment.

I replied with a dreamy-eyed "yes," to which she responded, "Why?" with a scrunched-up face that combined disgust and disbelief. *Surely she didn't know him as I did*, I thought. I turned around more fully to explain all the things I liked about him, including his smile, his eyes, his swagger, his football-playing physique, and a laundry list of other descriptors that Mariko, as evidenced by her eye-roll, found nauseating.

She looked me squarely in the eyes and said, "Girl, no," and then went on to describe the myriad of ways Alvin had been a douchebag in middle school in the "keep it real" way that only she could. At that moment, we became fast friends.

It had been seven years since we had spoken, and when she showed up at Al's funeral to pay her respects, I held back tears of joy at the sight of her. To this day, I can't really tell you why we didn't speak for that long. There was never a falling out—just a gradual losing touch. No matter the reason, I was so grateful she was there.

A few weeks later, we decided to grab coffee and catch up. Mariko was still living in the Bay Area, which made it easy for me to meet up with her near her home. We elected to sit at a table outside the coffee shop, which was the common COVID-19 protocol at the time.

At first, our conversation was tentative—with each of us feeling out the rhythm after not having connected in so long. But after the usual pleasantries and small talk about work and what we had been up to generally, our historical bond took over, and an ease set in.

Mariko reminded me of how often she, Al, and I used to hang out when he and I first got together. We had some hysterical nights out, including the time Al and I dressed up like Ike and Tina Turner for Halloween, and Mariko met up with us, and the three of us partied all night at the parade in San Francisco's Castro district.

Our conversation brought me back to the early days of Al's and my love story. It made me realize how much we had grown. Al and I were so young when we met, twenty-three and eighteen, respectively, and I was so naive. Reminiscing with her on the origins of our love made me feel closer to Al—and strangely, closer to myself. That day, Mariko helped me to remember who I was before my love journey with Al began.

The other friend who came back into my life around the time of Al's funeral was my friend Charo. Charo and I became friends in high school. There was a visible minority of students of color at our high school, so we naturally gravitated toward one another and became an extended clique of Black and Brown kids who ate lunch together in the student union.

Throughout high school, Charo, her sister Rowena, and me, along with a host of other girls, hung out almost every day. I used to love going to their house after school or coming by for family gatherings. During those gatherings, I got to experience some staples of Filipino culture, such as homemade lumpia, and karaoke in the living room. Those days of hanging out were the best.

A few months after Al died, the three of us reunited, and they took me out for drinks to take my mind off things—an act of care I desperately needed at the time. The girls continued to keep in touch with me and check in throughout the rest of that year.

By winter, I had settled more firmly into my work routine and was riding the recurring waves of stress like a Mavericks surfer. I was getting the urge to go out again and let my hair down. I wanted to have fun again. I missed hanging out with friends. And I missed having someone by my side through it all.

I've Got a Love Jones

By December 2021, I realized it was time for me to start going out more frequently and having fun. A couple of weeks before that revelation, I had admitted to my therapist how lonely I felt and how it would be nice to start dating again.

I was conducting that week's session from my car as I waited for my son to get his hair twisted. As soon as I uttered the words *I think I'm ready to date again*, I instantly felt butterflies in my stomach and wanted to swallow the words back whole. I felt a wave of shame rising in my chest as though I had done something wrong. Was I allowed to be with someone again? My heart was unsure.

"What you're feeling is totally normal," my therapist said. "It's normal to still have desires and a longing for connection."

Her words were comforting. I needed confirmation that my urge to connect with someone wasn't a betrayal.

"What would Al want for you?"

With tears welling up in my eyes, I responded instantly, "He would want me to be happy again."

I knew that to my core. Over the years, Al and I had that random and morbid conversation that many couples do, supposing what each would do if the other passed away. Every time we had this discussion, Al told me unequivocally that he would want me to find love again. He always said that if something happened to him, I deserved to be happy.

With my therapist's support—and some heavenly encouragement from Al, I suppose—I reluctantly opened my mind to the possibility of dating again. And as sure as the sunrise, the universe was right on time to offer some divine intervention.

It was Saturday, December 18, 2021, and Charo, Rowena, and I had agreed to meet up in Downtown Oakland for drinks that night. I was in my bathroom getting ready, trying to decide which outfit would make me look cute and approachable but not too thirsty.

I landed on a black scoop-neck sweater dress that showed a peek of cleavage but not too much. It was mid-length and had a slit up one side to my mid-thigh. With it being winter, I knew I couldn't go completely bare leg, so a pair of fishnet tights was my fashion-forward compromise. I finished off the look with a fitted leather motorcycle jacket and some leather ankle boots.

My hair was freshly done in wavy brown faux locks, and my makeup was on point. I had decided to go big on the eyes, my favorite facial feature, creating a cat-eye look with my gold glitter liner. A subtle pink gloss on my lips and a few dabs of blush, and I was ready to go . . . well, not so fast. As I glanced down, I noticed I was still wearing my wedding ring on my left hand.

It had been seven months since Al passed, and I hadn't taken my wedding ring off yet. I rubbed the ring gently with my right ring finger and thumb, conflicted about whether to leave it on or not. Then I felt a wave of calm come over me, and I knew it was time. I took off the ring and set it neatly in the jewelry tray on my bathroom counter. I then looked up and said aloud to the universe, "I'm open to whatever happens tonight."

I turned off my bathroom light, grabbed my purse, and hopped in my car, ready to have a great time.

We arrived at our first location of the night, a hipster-approved bar with an upstairs patio. We went upstairs and found a high table to sit at in the corner, out of the way of the twenty-somethings who occupied the space and looked younger than I remember looking at that age.

We decided to order some food from the pop-up restaurant downstairs that served Filipino food and the usual array of late-night munchies, including chicken wings, nachos, and fries. As we were waiting for our overpriced craft cocktails to show up, Charo took out her phone and began texting with a girlish grin that I hadn't seen since we were sixteen.

"Who are you texting with?" I asked, knowing it had to be someone good to have her so engrossed in her screen.

"My Boo," she grinned, looking up from her device at Rowena and me. "I was thinking about asking him to join us tonight." Charo and her "Boo" met on a dating app and had been casually dating for several weeks, seeing where things might go.

"Does Boo have some friends?" Rowena asked with a smirk.

I piled on with, "Yeah, Boo can come if he has some cute friends."

We laughed out loud in unison and continued to banter back and forth about bosses and kids and the dismal prospects of finding "the one" after forty in a sea of swipe-by-night dating apps.

"They're going to meet us at the next spot," Charo said. She was referring to Boo and his boys, who I hoped were at least fun company.

We closed out our tab and piled into Rowena's SUV to head five minutes away to the next bar on Broadway.

The three of us made it to the bar before the man who will forever be known as Boo and his friends arrived. As soon as we walked in, we noticed that this spot also had an outside patio, so we made a beeline for a high-top table and chairs on the right side of the outdoor space.

The patio was dimly lit, with rows of tea lights hung around the wooden rafters. There was a real tree adorned with lights sprouting proudly from the middle of the space. It was a surprising display of nature's glory in the middle of the urban jungle and created a cool, adult summer camp vibe.

Sitting outside was a great way to get fresh air and, we hoped, avoid catching COVID-19. But we quickly realized the patio heater nearest us wasn't working. And Jack Frost didn't care how cute we were in our assortment of little black dresses as he bellowed cold air our way.

Despite the frigid temp, I preferred to stay outside. Charo and Rowena were happy to oblige me and my sheltered immune system. So we zipped up our jackets and made plans to warm up by ordering another round of drinks.

By now, the patio was beginning to fill up, and I noticed a couple of guys hovering around the space as if they were waiting for someone. Within minutes, Charo's Boo arrived. Then he and the two guys I had noticed coalesced at our table.

The first guy to arrive was tall and slender with caramel-colored skin. He was wearing a red scarf under a long black coat that draped over his square shoulders. He immediately came and stood right next to me at the end of the table, where I sat on a high-back bar stool with my legs crossed tightly to keep in as much warmth as I could.

After a brief introduction, he leaned in toward me and said, "Here, take my gloves. You look cold." He handed me a pair of black wool gloves, which I happily placed on my hands. *That was sweet*, I thought. Tall guy earned some initial points with me for being observant and generous.

Meanwhile, Charo and her Boo were sitting across from us, engrossed in their own private world. He had his arm around her shoulder and was whispering something in her ear that made her burst into laughter. Her effervescent giggle was reminiscent of high school. The way their bodies turned in toward one another and the small touches back and forth signaled a level of comfort between them and an electric chemistry.

As we began to all converse as a group, I noticed that Boo's other friend remained pretty quiet. He elected to take a seat on the outskirts of the table, placing him behind me and kitty-corner to my left. Every now and then, he would add to the banter as we discussed musical tastes and a slew of other random topics while waiting for the bartender to refill our drinks.

Figuring him to be shy, I turned around and began chitchatting with him directly so he could be a part of the dialogue. I've always been sensitive to people being left out of a conversation. Although he was quiet, he radiated a powerful and self-assured energy that I picked up on immediately. It was as if his soul's Wi-Fi was turned on, and I was the only one attuned to its frequency.

After a brief exchange, I turned around, thinking nothing much about it other than he seemed like a really nice guy.

The frozen tundra, otherwise known as the patio, had taken its toll, and we were ready to move our bodies and our cocktails inside. The girls and I took this as an opportunity to go to the bathroom, touch up our lipstick, and spill the tea on what we thought about the guys.

"He's cute, Gina," Rowena said, referring to Tall Guy. "And I think he likes you."

"He seems cool," I replied with nonchalance. "We had a good conversation."

"What do you think of his friend, Wena? I think you two would be cute together," I told her as I blotted a paper towel on my freshly glossed lips. She quickly dismissed the idea and said to us that neither guy was her type, despite her sister and I secretly conspiring to hook her up the entire time.

Rowena was stunning but notoriously shy, which Charo and I worried could signal to some guys that she wasn't interested. Before we met up that night, Charo and I had made a pact that we would be her wing women—unbeknownst to her, of course. When the three of us returned from the bathroom, it was time to kick "Operation Hookup Rowena" into high gear.

I sashayed back to the bar area first, with the tipsy swagger of someone three drinks into an epic evening. Charo's Boo was at the bar ordering us some shots of mezcal. I could see Charo, Rowena, and Boo's other friend engaged in a lively conversation at the opposite end of the room.

I had walked up to Tall Guy, looking to rekindle our earlier conversation, but he was noticeably distracted and visibly uninterested in anything I had to say. "I'm going to go find the taco truck," he hollered to the other guys across the room. That was the final signal I needed that whatever fledgling connection we had on the patio was superseded by his need for late-night tacos.

I decided to join the conversation Charo and Rowena were having with the other friend. It was at that point that I learned that friend number two was named Jeff. Although I'm sure he told me that earlier, I usually have to hear someone's name twice before it sticks.

When we asked what he did for a living, Jeff told us he did freelance graphic design and was a music artist. I could see his eyes beaming as he shared his latest accomplishment: having one of his original songs featured in the CW television show *All American*. The way he spoke so passionately about his music was alluring.

From that point on, I began to notice his chestnut brown eyes and neatly groomed beard. Jeff was average height, with a stocky build. He was wearing a stylish brown fedora, a button-down shirt the color of orange sherbet, tan slacks, and brown leather shoes to match. Jeff was handsome, and most importantly, I could sense that he was a genuinely nice guy.

However, this mission is about Rowena, I reminded myself internally. But it was clear that Rowena was not interested in Jeff, judging by her body language. And he had not made any overt gestures toward her. I decided I'd sit back and observe the dynamics a bit more to see where things might go.

After we finished our shots of mezcal, it was time for our group to head to the next location, a trendy club in Downtown Oakland that played hip-hop on Saturday nights. As we were leaving, we waved goodbye to Tall Guy, heading off in search of his taco truck, and Jeff and I slid into the back of Rowena's SUV parked out front.

Rowena didn't know exactly where we were headed, so she called Charo, who was riding in the car with her Boo. As they aligned on directions, Jeff and I made small talk in the back seat.

Suddenly, Jeff grabbed my right hand with his left fingers interlaced between mine and said, "I like your nails." I had a gel manicure with black, white, and gold geometric shapes on each finger. I didn't have time to get my nails done that week, so I applied one of those stick-on manicures that had become popular during the pandemic.

Jeff held up my right hand as if he were Picasso admiring his artwork under the moonlight. As soon as our fingers interlaced, I felt a spark between us. Not the spark you get from static electricity, either. This was a spark that made me feel instantly connected to him. The kind that if I stared long enough, I might see our life together unfolding in his eyes.

He must have felt something, too, because we locked eyes in unison and smiled before turning away. Before we could explore this sudden connection any further, it was time to get out. Rowena had found a parking spot around the corner from the club.

By the time we arrived at the club, I realized that I had already tiptoed past tipsy. But that didn't stop me from joining the others at the bar for another round of shots. I figured one more drink couldn't hurt, especially since I planned to dance it off.

The club was long and narrow. Upon entering, there was a small area the size of a dorm room where people could gather beside the bar. Past the bar, to the right was a larger area in the back where there was a sweaty mosh pit of twenty-somethings twerking in front of the DJ.

We decided to hang out in the front section, where there was at least partial ventilation. I was standing off to the side of the bar, bouncing ever so slightly as I started to feel the music. Charo was talking with her Boo near the bar, and Rowena was standing near me, trying not to be approached by any of the drunk guys passing by.

I was not as lucky. Before I could repel anyone with a stank look on my face, a guy came up to me and started grinding his body against me as I was dancing near the wall. This guy was aggressive and sweaty. It was as if he just came off the football field after scoring a touchdown and had walked right into the club.

I was desperate not to be his two-point conversion, but I was rusty at curving guys at a club. After all, this was my return to the draft after being with the same team for twenty-one years. As he continued to try to press his body against mine, I stood there dancing awkwardly for a couple of minutes, trying to figure out what to do next.

I quickly scanned the club, and as my head turned to the left, I could see Jeff standing against the wall near the entrance. We locked eyes instantly. Thank goodness he was looking in my direction! I knew I needed some help getting this creep off me. Instinctively, I looked at Jeff and mouthed the words, "HELP ME."

With zero hesitation, Jeff walked over, hugged me tightly, and pulled me away from the sweaty guy, who was seething with disbelief. I hugged him back even tighter and whispered, "Thank you," in his ear. We quickly called out to the rest of our crew, letting them know it was time to go. Then Jeff and I walked out of the club holding hands, giggling like two kids who had stolen a cookie from the jar and gotten away with it.

Whoever said chivalry is dead had not encountered this marvelous man. We continued talking and holding hands for a few blocks until we made it to Rowena's car. As we stopped at the corner and looked into each other's eyes, I could feel the electric current running between us. At that moment, despite everything I had gone through, I couldn't help but wonder if this was the spark of something spectacular.

SEVEN

Reinvention

"I'm at an inflection point. I can either build or burn.
I can embrace the pain or run . . . I can either break
or bend . . . or take one step, each day, to the top."
—MY JOURNAL, 7.27.21

"Come down and give me a hug," I yelled up the stairs to Morgan as I dragged my well-worn, red Tumi hard case down the steps and into the living room. In what seemed like ten long teenage minutes, he finally appeared, looking like he just rolled out of bed—which no doubt he had, despite it being almost noon.

Morgan stood in the living room facing me, his head encroaching on the open doorframe of the hallway. I couldn't believe how tall my baby had gotten. At sixteen and nearly six foot four, it seemed silly to still call him my baby. But like all mothers will attest, their kid will forever be a child in their eyes. And besides, Morgan still had a baby face like a cherub but with the smug expression of the internet sensation Grumpy Cat.

"Can you put my luggage in the car, Boo?" (I had been calling him Boo since he was a toddler.)

"Okay," he said with a groan, bending down to grab the suitcase.

"Now remember, I'll be gone for two days. I'm heading up to Sonoma for a spa trip. Don't forget to feed and walk Rocket."

"All right," he said with a look of annoyance from having heard that last part a few times already in the week leading up to today.

Even though my sister Kea would be home with him, I still felt the need to remind Morgan of his responsibilities to help her out. After a few more goodbyes and I love you's to Kea, Morgan, and Rocket, I was in the car headed for Sonoma Wine Country.

It was New Year's Day, and I was amazed at how light the traffic was driving up to Sonoma. I arrived in a little over an hour and couldn't wait to check in, drop my bags in the room, and get to my massage appointment. I had decided to book an overnight stay at the Fairmont Sonoma Mission Inn to ring in 2022 in luxurious style.

As I walked to my appointment in my freshly laundered spa robe, I marveled at the ornate doorknobs and antique paintings that adorned the hallways. The grounds of the hotel were breathtaking, with lush trees and vegetation creating a protective thicket to hide the beauty of this place from the rest of the world. It reminded me of a quaint Spanish villa with a touch of midcentury Hollywood glam.

I was told to check in for my appointment at the spa gift shop. This was no doubt a clever ploy to get me to buy more spa goodies, which was inevitable, as I scanned the shop with my eyes lit up like a Las Vegas slot machine.

The gift shop attendant was lovely. After explaining the process, she gave me a tour of the spa area, including the women's locker room, then walked me over to my appointment. As we walked down a beautiful spiral stone staircase, I took in the crisp afternoon air. I noticed a couple swimming in the turquoise blue pool in the shape of a lucky clover. Next to them were rows of mostly empty pool chairs.

When we arrived at the bottom of the stone staircase, I saw a section of poolside cabanas draped in flowy white linens. The cabanas were roped off in a private area that was empty. I imagined that come summer, those cabanas would be overflowing with an assortment of Real Housewife types.

The spa attendant led me into the spa area of the resort, and my mouth nearly fell open. Just beyond the reception desk was a spacious waiting area decorated with dark-gray rattan furniture surrounding a floor-to-ceiling abstract white sculpture that resembled a waterfall. The entire space looked like the pages of a West Elm catalog.

However, the pièce de résistance was the mineral baths. To the left of the waiting area was a large opening that led to the mineral pool with water from the surrounding Boyes Hot Springs. I learned that an entire wellness ritual went along with the mineral bath. And since I had time to kill before my massage, I thought, *Why not try it out?*

The spa receptionist handed me a laminated card with all the steps, which began with using one of the surrounding showers to rinse off with one of their organic exfoliating scrubs. However, you could choose the order of your experience—whichever combination of shower, mineral bath, and sauna you prefer.

I scanned the room and was surprised to see that this area was coed. There were four or five couples already there, plus a few solo women like myself. I felt awkward at first, having not experienced anything this luxurious before. And I couldn't help but notice that there weren't any other Black people there, which made it hard not to feel out of place. But I put my initial discomfort at bay, disrobed to my swimsuit, and melted into the eighty-degree waters of the hot springs. *What a way to kick off 2022 and release the pain of last year,* I thought! *A girl could get used to this.*

The Pleasure Principles

To say that 2021 was the worst year of my life would be the laugh-out-loud understatement of the century. The pain I had suffered from the loss of my husband left me spinning aimlessly for most of that year. I had been sucker-punched in the stomach, and by December, I was just getting myself off the mat.

Actually, by the end of the year, I was doing much better than just standing up. I had been doing more with family and friends, taking better care of myself, and I'd even met someone new who caught my interest. A spark inside had begun to flicker, and my spirit had come alive again.

I had begun to move through life differently. When I was at the height of my grief, I couldn't imagine life going on most days. It was hard to imagine a future for myself beyond the loss I had endured. I was convinced that every day of my life moving forward was going to be stained with longing for the life that had vanished—for the life I dreamed I'd spend growing old with my husband.

Yet, somewhere along the way in 2021, I found hope. My soul had come to an acceptance of sorts that if I was still here on this earthly trek, my life was too precious to waste. I now understand all too clearly how life ebbs and flows and can change dramatically in an instant, so it's best to seize it and squeeze every drop of pleasure out of it you can!

It was with this mindset that some renewed principles for living were born. I didn't want to go back to the darkness and pain that had engulfed me the year prior. I couldn't live like that anymore. My spirit had experienced joy again, and I was holding on for dear life. As I was relaxing and reflecting on my journey of recovery in my hotel room in Sonoma, I made a pact with myself to live this year to the fullest.

I decided that this year I'd be open to any and everything that brought me joy. I began to try and do so many new things—some I'd always wanted to do more of, like travel, but didn't make time for because of various demands or because I just couldn't afford to. I set out to do what brought me joy as much as possible in 2022, and by the end of that year, what had emerged were three new principles, or general instructions, for how I would approach life moving forward:

- **Principle 1:** Give yourself permission to **indulge.**
- **Principle 2:** Embrace new **adventures.**
- **Principle 3:** Say many more nos to **make space for the juicy yeses!**

My mini spa staycation in Sonoma was the first 2022 experience of allowing myself to indulge. But this was a small luxury compared to the over-the-top birthday party I had been planning for myself, now just six weeks away.

Permission to Have Fun

"This space will be perfect!" I told Stacy, the event planner for the venue I was interested in. A few months prior to my Sonoma trip, in the fall of 2021, my sister Kea and I had begun scoping out venues for my birthday extravaganza. This space in Oakland was the second location we visited, and I was in love with it.

The first venue we looked at was in San Francisco, and it was gorgeous, but it was too difficult to locate, and parking was nonexistent. But this venue was near Oakland's Jack London Square with plenty of parking, and the vibe was just right. It had ten thousand square feet of open space, a stage for the DJ, a catering kitchen, and a full bar. I asked Stacy to draw up the agreement that day. I was ready to sign.

Now that I had the venue settled, it was time to finalize the catering and figure out how to decorate the space. It had been five months since Al died, and I was still very much grieving the loss. But I knew I needed a healthy distraction, which planning this party had become.

Aside from being a useful diversion, this birthday party was a wish fulfilled for Al and me. A few years prior, Al told me he wanted to throw me a massive party for my fortieth birthday. Unfortunately, he didn't get to do so because we were in the midst of COVID-19. But we were both about to get our wish.

Now that vaccines were in place and COVID-19 precautions were in effect nearly everywhere, I felt it would be a great time to throw myself the birthday party he and I had always wanted, albeit for forty-one—or "Forty: One More Time," as I coined it.

Over the course of that fall, I was busy planning every detail of the party, from the guest list, photo booth, gold-colored place settings, balloon structures, and much more, including my outfits—multiple outfit changes for this soiree were a must. As you can probably tell, I spared almost no expense to make every detail special. One of my friends was convinced I was planning a wedding for myself. I had never held a party this grand before, but if any year of my life warranted a celebration after the loss I had suffered, this was for sure the one.

My family and friends certainly agreed. They offered to help in any way possible. My sister helped me select the perfect menu with the caterer. My mom helped with venue selection, and my cousin Dana made the most decadent-smelling candles for me to hand out as party favors. It turned out to be a true family affair.

I was engrossed in party planning when another idea flashed into my mind.

"What if I do a dance routine!" I said to my sister one day.

"What? Like a flash mob?" Kea asked with a look somewhere between confusion and disbelief that my forty-year-old knees could survive such a feat.

"Sort of. I could hire a group of dancers, and we could do a performance like I used to do on dance troupe." I was so giddy at the thought that I could hardly contain myself.

"Where are you going to find dancers?" she asked, puzzled.

"I can look on IG or reach out to some local dance studios. It's going to be so dope. It'll be a surprise performance that no one is expecting!"

"You are so extra," Kea said as she rolled her eyes and laughed out loud.

I couldn't help but laugh, too. She's right. I was extra, over the top, or whatever other synonym for being bold and doing the most. I have always loved to dance. I was captain of my high school dance team, and my secret dream career was to travel the world as a backup dancer for Janet Jackson.

The idea of hiring dancers to perform a choreographed dance routine with me at my party would require a lot of time and hard work on my part. But I couldn't think of anything more blissful and on-brand for me than that. Challenge accepted!

By the second week of January, rehearsals with the dancers were in full swing. I decided to partner with Paradise Dance Studio in the Bay Area, which is owned and managed by a talented dancer and choreographer named Kyra. After a lovely meet and greet, Kyra and I settled on a plan for her to choreograph a short hip-hop routine that she and her assistant would perform alongside me at my party.

When the night of the party finally arrived, I was on pins and needles with excitement. I had just arrived at the venue, and after doing a quick scan to survey the scene to ensure the setup was on track, I made a beeline for the changing room on the mezzanine level to lay out my evening looks—three outfits to be exact.

After I stashed my stuff, I walked out into the open balcony area. There were a few armchairs scattered throughout and a black metal railing leading down the staircases on either side. I looked over and saw the hustle and bustle of the event staff putting their finishing touches on linens, balloon fixtures, audio equipment, and lights. Pretty soon, it would be showtime!

The first two hours of my birthday party went by in a flash. I spent most of that time greeting my guests, many of whom hadn't been to a large event since the pandemic began. I was so grateful they all decided to come out to celebrate with me, including those friends who flew in from out of town.

When it was time, I quietly made my way upstairs to slip into my second outfit of the night, a black sequined romper with a black tulle skirt and dance shoes with a four-inch heel that I had thankfully broken in over the six weeks of grueling rehearsals leading up to the event.

The three of us managed to assemble in a line along the stairs on the right side of the mezzanine without too many people noticing us. My nerves were doing backflips as I closed my eyes to recount every eight count I had meticulously studied with them. I felt like I was preparing for a final exam. For a split second, I panicked. *What am I doing? What if I break my ankle in these four-inch heels? What if I miss a step? I'm forty-one, not the seventeen-year-old dance captain I once was. This is wild!*

But there was no turning back now. I glanced up at the heavens, hoping Al was watching over me at that moment, cheering me on. I then looked over at the DJ, which was our signal to start the music and for the venue to dim the lights. And then, on cue, we heard Beyoncé's sultry voice blaring from the speakers and the beat drop for her song "Shining," produced by DJ Khaled. At that moment, my guests realized what was happening, and the crowd went wild, clapping and screaming for us at the top of their lungs.

Surrounded by my family and closest friends, I realized that, just like DJ Khaled says at the beginning of the song, I had been waiting my whole life to find an excuse to celebrate the triumph of being unapologetically me.

We killed the performance. But more importantly, I ended that night so happy and incredibly proud for allowing myself to fully indulge in every drop of love, laughter, and lightness that life had to offer.

Learning to let my hair down and indulge even my wackiest ideas was one of the first true aha moments of 2022. My birthday party taught me that it's okay to do something special for myself just because. It reminded me that I have agency in how I live my life. That no matter what tragedy has happened and will happen to me in the future, I can choose joy.

I know how fortunate I was to have the financial means to indulge in this way, and I realize that not everybody can afford to splurge. However, there are still ways to enjoy intentional moments of bliss in your life at every price point. It could be as simple as calling up a few girlfriends and taking that trap yoga class you've been meaning to try.

Following my birthday party on February 19, 2022, I wore my newfound joy like a badge of honor and began to cultivate it in all areas of my life. I had reawakened to life and was on a quest to discover new experiences. Lucky for me, the universe happily gave me what I asked. Less than a month after my party, I was on a plane headed to Mexico to spend the weekend with my new beau.

Adventure Time

"I can't believe we're actually here," I said to Jeff as we sat on the patio of the rooftop bar of our hotel.

"Right? Me either!" he said, his smile beaming as we held each other's hands across the tiny white bistro table.

It was a beautiful day in March, and we had just arrived in Puerto Vallarta an hour earlier to spend the weekend there for Jeff's birthday. It was a relatively quick flight, around three and a half hours from the Bay Area. After a busy day of travel and weeks of anticipation, we were ready for a drink. The rooftop bar seemed like an excellent place to start our tropical mini vacay.

While we waited for the bartender to bring our cocktails, Jeff and I basked in the afternoon sun, enjoying each other's company. We were seated next to a long glass bar that ran almost the full length of the patio. In the middle of the patio was a stunning infinity pool that overlooked Banderas Bay with a clear view of the Pacific Ocean on the horizon. Jeff and I agreed that we had to get in the pool before the night was over.

There were other couples and groups of friends scattered about the patio. Some were taking a dip in the pool. Others were lounging in beach chairs along the perimeter or outstretched in daybeds and cabanas that anchored each corner of the space. Jeff and I remained seated at our bistro table, eyes locked on each other, relaxing in a mutual vibe of "go with the flow."

This was definitely a first for me. Not only was this my first trip to Puerto Vallarta, but it also was my first time out of the country with a man I was still getting to know. It seems unbelievable when I look back at it now, but we booked this trip to Puerto Vallarta in January, just six weeks after we met.

The whole idea for the trip started as a casual conversation with friends over late-night Chinese food the night that we met. After arriving at separate times in separate vehicles, he and I wound up sitting next to each other at the large round table the six of us occupied.

By this point in the evening, we were more comfortable with each other, so the conversation flowed easily. He told me more about his family, including the fact that he had a daughter. I told him about my son, Morgan, and shared with him that I was a recent widow.

Something about his kind demeanor and the ease of the conversation made me instantly comfortable opening up to him. I paused for a minute after telling him about Al, not sure of how he'd react. But without skipping a beat, his eyes softened with compassion, and he said, "Aw, I'm so sorry to hear that." And then we continued our conversation. He made me feel normal at that moment—not like being widowed was this awkward or fragile thing to be avoided.

One of our friends at the table brought up the topic of travel. I asked Jeff if he liked to travel, and he responded yes and that he needed to get some more stamps on his passport. I told him that I had a few stamps from work travel but definitely wanted more and was dying to go to the Caribbean. We joked as a group that we should keep the party going by booking a friends trip to Tulum or Turks and Caicos. Jeff said he was down, and I said I was too. He then yelled across the table, "Who's going to book it?"

Charo responded, "You boys have to plan it." We all erupted in laughter, knowing we had a better chance of winning the lottery than these guys planning a proper trip without our help.

A few weeks later, Jeff and I were talking on the phone one afternoon. "What's up with that trip?" he asked.

"Are you serious? You really want to go somewhere?"

"Yeah, I'd love to go on a trip."

"Well, I could ask Charo and Rowena if they're interested. Do you think your friends will be able to come?"

We discussed potential options for a group trip. After talking through the pros and cons of going as a group, we landed on going to Puerto Vallarta together—just the two of us. We decided that the second weekend of March would be the perfect romantic getaway for his birthday. It was already mid-January, though, so we had to make arrangements fast.

This became our first project as a new couple, one that could have exposed potential cracks in our fledgling union. Instead, we worked together effortlessly on planning the trip. We divided and conquered while making joint decisions where needed. He booked the hotel, and I took care of the flights. That same effortless partnership that got everything booked on short notice carried over to carefree vibes throughout the four-day trip. The restorative experience of our care-free vacation became the impetus for pleasure principle number two: embrace new adventures.

Although I was stress-free the entire time I was there, I knew my family was freaking out back home, so I made it a point to reach out to them each day to let them know I was okay. I remember Morgan's reaction when I told him I was going on a trip with the guy I had just started seeing.

"What? That's crazy," Morgan responded.

"I know it sounds crazy, but everything will be fine. I've been to Mexico before, and I know how to get myself back home in an emergency." I gave Morgan a look of assurance, knowing full well I couldn't explain or transpose my intuition that I was safe anywhere in the world with Jeff. I knew in my soul that he would do everything in his power to protect me.

With his signature snarky style, Morgan countered, "Okay, don't get murdered."

I fired back an equally sarcastic response. "You do know it'd be easier for him to harm me here on American soil." A bit of dark humor, but underneath it all, a sweet show of concern from my son, who couldn't help but worry about his mom.

The four days that Jeff and I spent in Puerto Vallarta were magical. We did the typical tourist attractions, such as taking a boat to an artificial island in the middle of Banderas Bay for a Cirque du Soleil-style show. But we also ventured off the resort to explore Zona Romántica and immerse ourselves in the local culture. Time seemed to stand still as we walked along the Malecon Boardwalk that day, taking pictures and people-watching, observing the sun-kissed bodies milling around us.

Our hotel accommodations felt even more like a fairy tale. Jeff had gotten lucky and booked us the last corner suite on one of the highest floors, so we had a breathtaking view. Our resort was perched atop a hillside with a view of the entire Bay and the Pacific Ocean from our wraparound balcony.

Our balcony could have had its own zip code. One side had a view of the hillside and led directly into the bedroom. When we walked around the corner of the balcony, we were immediately transported to our own personal paradise, complete with a hammock, lounge chairs, and a massive hot tub with an unobstructed view of the ocean through the glass railing.

For all the years that Al and I were together, we were never able to travel like this. At the beginning of our relationship, we just couldn't afford it. And then life settled in, and work, and obligations, and Morgan's sports, and all the things conspired to keep us firmly on California soil.

During the pandemic, we daydreamed of traveling abroad after Morgan went off to college. Being on the balcony of this beautiful resort in Puerto Vallarta was not only a dream deferred for me, but a dream fulfilled for Al, as his memory and spirit still occupied my heart.

On the morning before our last day there, I woke up early to get in some morning yoga on the balcony. As I moved through my beginner Vinyasa flow, I soaked up the sun's rays and life's budding possibilities. I couldn't believe I was there. As I reflected on the blessing of it all, I grabbed my digital notepad to journal the feelings I couldn't quite name but couldn't contain.

Just then, Jeff came out to join me on the balcony. "Hey, beautiful, good morning," he said as he stepped into the hot tub.

"Hey, babe, good morning. I'm just doing some morning stretches."

"Don't mind me, baby. Keep doing your thing." The depth of his tone, deep and rich like molasses, overshadowed the birds singing their morning arias.

I continued to journal for a few more minutes before closing my eyes to meditate. I was more relaxed than I had been in years. Before Al died, it seemed as though I was always rushing. He used to beg me to slow down and relax. Now, on the balcony of this resort, I couldn't even tell you what all the rushing was for. I realized at that moment that I always had the ability to hit the pause button, find a quiet space, and soak life in.

The trip to Puerto Vallarta showed me that life is full of big adventures if you're open to embracing them. And within those big adventures, it's just as important to embrace the quiet moments and claim your peace as I did on the balcony. Now that I understood that I had the power to manifest experiences like this in my everyday life, there was nothing left to do but create more space for big living.

Make Space for Yes

Although 2022 was off to an amazing start, and I was feeling more hopeful than ever, there was one area of my life I was still struggling with—my career. Don't get me wrong, I was still performing well at work and had established a reputation as a respected leader on the DEI team. However, increasingly I was becoming disillusioned with corporate life.

The more I leaned into a life of ease and adventure, the more I seemed to be at odds with the constraints of a nine-to-five filled with meetings and never-ending workstreams. I longed for freedom and the ability to work my own way when I preferred to work on projects that truly mattered.

I was approaching my second year at Meta and my eighteenth year as an HR practitioner, and the fire I once had to climb the corporate ladder continuously was like a waning candle or a slow ember. Losing Al so suddenly fundamentally shifted my motivation for working. It was no longer about proving myself or chasing a six-figure paycheck. I now craved a career where I could fulfill my deepest purpose, which I now believed was transforming other women to live more in alignment with themselves the way I had learned to do.

Truth be told, I knew long before Al died that the corporate rat race was slowly sucking my soul, but I didn't have the courage to step away from it nor the role models or resources to make entrepreneurship a reality. However, Al's passing opened a portal to a new universe—a realm where I was not afraid to take risks or embrace the bossy, badass woman I am on the inside!

With that epiphany, I began ignoring the frequent attempts by external recruiters to connect me with new opportunities. Before then, I would entertain certain roles that seemed interesting or ones that could be a potential next step in my career. During the first half of 2022, I had numerous recruiters contact me, and I had even gone through some initial interviews for head of DEI-type roles.

But it was clear to me now that what I really wanted was the creative freedom to run my own business. And no matter how good the job description or the salary sounded, I would be leaving Meta for another corporate job that promised much of the same things: burnout, boredom, or bureaucracy.

In July, just as I had made up my mind to no longer pursue other jobs and instead focus on my role at Meta until I was ready to make a permanent transition, a tempting opportunity came across my inbox. A search firm reached out to me for a unique opportunity as VP of Diversity, Equity, and Inclusion for a small, mission-driven software company. I was instantly intrigued. I was generally familiar with the company, but surprised to learn that they had a strong philanthropic arm and were investing heavily in underserved communities, which completely aligned with my values.

After a successful first round of interviews, the company was ready to advance me to the final stage. A part of me really wanted the role. I felt a connection with the hiring manager, and I knew I could come in and make progress on their most pressing DEI challenges. But a voice inside me said, *Is this what you really want?* I knew it wasn't. A part of my ego still wanted to prove I could do it and even check off the accomplishment of reaching the VP level in my career. Luckily, all the lessons I had learned over the past year came to the surface and drowned out my wavering ego stuck at an imaginary crossroads.

The choice was clear. I contacted the search firm the next day and told them I was withdrawing my candidacy.

That same week, I had a serendipitous encounter with a distant neighbor that solidified my decision. Each day I typically walked my dog along the same route, which involved traveling down a tree-lined pathway that connected my neighborhood to the adjacent one. Coming out of the narrow pathway was a well-kept, two-story black-and-white house at the end of a cul-de-sac. As I approached the house on my way to the nearby park, I recognized the tall blonde woman walking my way as one of the friendly neighbors Al had always stopped to talk to on his walks with Rocket. She had two small dogs that despised every other canine but, for some reason, took a liking to Rocket.

I had seen her a few times since Al passed. She was one of the first neighbors to ask about him after he died because she hadn't seen him walking Rocket for a few days. She and I always spoke when we saw each other, but for the life of me, I could never remember her name. I am notoriously bad with names, but I never forget a face.

When we ran into each other this morning, we quickly moved past the normal pleasantries and began discussing work. I asked her to remind me of her name, and she told me it was Misty. *That's right! I knew it started with an M.* Misty shared that, like me, she worked from home and had been in the tech industry before leaving her job to start her own business. My ears immediately perked up. I asked her if she'd be open to a cup of coffee so I could pick her brain on how she made the leap out of corporate.

It was like the universe was waiting for me to declare what I wanted so it could offer me all the resources and information I needed, starting with this unexpected encounter with Misty. We exchanged numbers, and I reached out later that day to schedule our coffee talk.

Misty and I met up for coffee in early August 2022. We laughed about some of the situations we had encountered in the wonderfully wacky world of tech. I was fascinated by her business, which consisted of using theater skills to teach executive women public speaking skills. Her passion was contagious, and I loved hearing about the freedom and fulfillment she had in serving her dedicated tribe of amazing women.

Misty had mentioned that she was writing a book with the help of a book coach. I told her that it was also a dream of mine, and she offered to send me her coach's information. Her coach, Stacy Ennis, would eventually become my coach and guide for the book you're reading today.

What seemed like a series of random events and information was actually what I believe to have been a spiritual fulfillment of my heart's desires. The caveat was that these desires could only come to pass once I declared them out loud and made space in my life for them to manifest.

You see if I had continued my pattern of jumping from one job to the next, chasing more status or more zeros on my paycheck, I would have cemented the status quo. Instead, I decided to close the door on another job and open the door to a future of my design. Saying no to the software company and no to the idea of staying in corporate created space for me to write this book and live the life of my dreams.

New Routines

My new principles for living would have remained just that—principles—unless I was able to incorporate them into my normal life.

Fortunately for me, translating these principles into patterns of behavior happened organically.

When it came to living **Principle 1,** my newfound mantra of **"Give yourself permission to indulge,"** these are the behaviors that reinforced it:

- Treating myself to good coffee from a coffee shop whenever I feel like it—at least once a week to get out of the house
- Periodically going out for frozen yogurt, especially after a long day working from home
- Purchasing as many books as my heart desires, even if I have no more room on my shelves
- Splurging on luxury lipsticks despite having nearly every color to complement any outfit
- Sleeping in past 8:00 a.m. on weekends
- Allowing myself twenty-four hours of no responsibility a week. (This one is my favorite!) This means someone else is on dinner duty, walking the dog, or figuring out how to unclog the sink while I relax and do nothing or everything—whatever I decide is on my agenda!

Living out **Principle 2: Embrace new adventures** became an exciting challenge. For me, new adventures meant traveling to new places or going on interesting dates or meetups with friends. The following are some ways this principle currently is manifested in my life:

- Picking at least one new travel destination a year
- Dining at new restaurants or trying new dishes at my favorite places
- Changing my hair often to experiment with new looks
- Attending music festivals and concerts in different cities

- Being open to conversation when I'm out and about to learn new things from new people

Principle 3: Say many more nos to make space for the juicy yeses! was perhaps the hardest for me to implement regularly. I think it has a lot to do with the fact that I'm an optimist, and I get excited by possibility. This means that I hate to turn down an opportunity for fear of missing out on something. But what life has recently taught me is that you must be willing to close a door for another door, usually the better one, to open. The following are some of the ways I began to live out saying no and making space:

- Turning down extra assignments at work that didn't add long-term value (i.e., "busy work")

- Delegating more chores and tasks around the house to my son or my sister to allow me to relax or work on my business

- Ignoring LinkedIn messages and emails about job opportunities

- Turning down unpaid speaking engagements or conference attendance to make space for paid opportunities that are in line with the business and brand I'm building

Another way I've categorized my new routines is through the lens of timing. Some things I do daily, some routines are weekly, and others occur on a quarterly or even annual basis. Here are a few examples of how these routines play out over the course of a calendar year:

Daily Routines

- Getting some form of movement every day. Stretching counts!

- Going inward and connecting with myself for at least five minutes in the morning before starting work

- Ending work by 5:00 p.m. most days
- Taking a shower and listening to music before bed
- Reading or journaling to wind down

Weekly Routines

- Working out two or three times a week
- Grabbing coffee from my favorite coffee shop on Fridays
- Having twenty-four hours with no responsibility every week
- Texting or calling family and friends to check in

Monthly Routines

- Buying myself flowers a couple of times a month
- Attending a music event or going dancing
- Binge-watching a new show or going to a movie

Quarterly Routines

- Going on a weekend getaway or weeklong vacation to unwind
- Getting a massage

Annual Routines

- Taking a solo trip to reflect and plan my intentions for the coming year
- Cleaning out my closet and donating clothes to a women's shelter

These routines keep me anchored in caring for myself and honoring my mental, physical, and emotional needs. Now, as I'm writing this more than a year out from my day at the spa, I'm grateful for the whimsical year of new experiences that shifted my existence from dejected, fractured, and grieving to happy, whole, and healed.

EIGHT

Welcome Home

*"We experience the world in the ways we need
to grow. Pain is an exploration of what's buried
within. Joy is a reminder that pain does end."*

—MY JOURNAL, 11.5.21

As I sit here writing this book, nearly two years after my husband passed away, I have such a profound appreciation for my journey and the hard-won peace and clarity I have arrived at in life. I've learned so many lessons about myself, life, the grace of the Creator, and the endurance of the human spirit.

I've learned that life takes you where you need to go to evolve, which is often far from where you thought you were headed. I spent years climbing the corporate ladder with my foot on the gas pedal, determined to make it to the top. And yes, I did, in fact, achieve extraordinary success in my career, landing an executive role at one of the most profitable and arguably most influential companies that ever existed. But the climb was steep. And the cost was even more immense.

I achieved what most people can only dream of achieving, especially women of color who come from marginalized communities like I did. However, I paid the toll at every step along the journey with sweat, tears, illness, anxiety, disillusionment, and burnout. After years of suffering on the inside while projecting outward success, I now know you can't ignore the whispers for long.

I have come to realize that a blueprint for success that requires self-sacrifice and total allegiance to something other than your own inner wisdom is a dead end. This blueprint is especially outdated for women whose energy and resources are also overtaxed outside of work in caring for their families and communities. For women of color, add the emotional toll of code-switching, dodging microaggressions, and outright bias, as well as the pressure of often being the financial support for immediate and extended family. All of this has led me to conclude that our modern-day hustle culture and toxic busyness are unsustainable and unfulfilling for all of us.

Now, that doesn't mean that you can't work in service of a corporation or institution. You do not need to vacate your leadership position or start over from scratch in your career to enact the lessons in this book. However, you do have to embrace a new way of operating in the world. You must *reconnect with your heart* so you can hear its desires. You must *restore your body*, so you have the strength and vigor to pursue your dreams. You'll need to *reframe your beliefs* from self-sacrifice to self-worth. You must *renew your spirit* by tapping in deeply to uncover and honor what brings you joy. And you'll need to *reinvent your routines* and embed these new, self-sustaining practices into your daily life.

The MeaningFULL Life Method

As I've illustrated, I did not arrive at joy, meaning, or purpose overnight. In fact, as I shared earlier in the book, I didn't even want to carry on with life because I was so shattered by my loss. *But it's the whispers of life that keep us going.* As I mentioned in Chapter 1, I was conditioned to ignore the whispers like so many of us are. I believe we all receive the whispers or nudges from our spirit or subconscious that signal to us when there's a problem. And as I learned, if you listen hard enough, those whispers also contain the solution.

For instance, in the weeks and months after Al died, I didn't even want to get out of bed. I could only muster enough energy to walk my dog each morning and then find a convenient space in my house to crawl back into my shell of grief alone. But one morning, I heard a whisper from my spirit to get out of bed and stretch, which led to me discovering Kundalini yoga, and this helped me cope with my anxiety and gave me something to look forward to and challenge myself with each day.

Throughout this book, I've shared my personal stories to illustrate that it's possible to come through hell and thrive on the other side. However, as I outlined in Chapter 2, it does take **space** to reflect, the passage of **time**, some **intention**, and most importantly, **YOU** to show up for yourself to seize your meaningFULL life.

In the pages that follow, I'll summarize the key lessons of my method from each chapter, along with some additional tips you can use to design or rebuild a fuller, more meaningful life.

Reconnect with Your Heart

In Chapter 3, I revealed how difficult it was for me to tap into my grief and sorrow because I had been conditioned to be a "Strong Black Woman" for most of my life, which meant holding it together no matter what. Being raw and emotionally vulnerable was not part of the script. And neither was rest.

Until Instagram head Adam Mosseri nudged me to take the time I needed, it never dawned on me to even ask for more time to heal. And thankfully, I listened because it gave me time to get away from the sadness that permeated my home and visit my brother and his family in Los Angeles, where I was smothered with love.

That summer, I also took the opportunity to go on a solo vacation. It was the first time in my life I went away by myself, not counting business trips. And unlike a business trip, my itinerary in Mendocino was all my own. That trip, taken just two months after Al passed, was the first chance I had to pause and take a breath. I needed that space away from my day-to-day life to think and make sense of everything I was going through.

My time away also allowed for a serendipitous encounter with some lovely strangers at a local restaurant. That day I had actively avoided leaving my room and had made several attempts just to stay there and eat junk food in my pajamas. But the universe was having none of it! I ended up running out of food and had to go out to get myself something to eat, which led me to dine with two fellow grief-stricken humans and a conversation I'll never forget.

When it comes to **reconnecting with your heart**, here are the lessons I learned that summer:

- **Accept help.** Whether it was Adam encouraging me to take time, my friends and family providing food for us, or my brother offering extra love and support, the underlying gesture was the same. People saw I needed help and gave freely of their time, money, love, and support. And perhaps because I was too wounded to put up a fuss, I welcomed and relished the help for the first time in my life. Ultimately, that experience taught me to be willing to accept support in the future whenever I need it and, most importantly, not to be afraid to ask for help.

- **Don't be afraid to feel.** There's a familiar adage that says, "You have to feel it to heal it." I couldn't agree more. I had suppressed or ignored strong feelings for most of my life. But Al's death was like the tidal wave of emotions that finally broke the levee wall. Through individual therapy, journaling, and embracing tiny moments of joy, like watching my niece have fun on the beach in San Diego, I slowly began to identify and reconnect with my emotions. Once I acknowledged and allowed myself to feel the feelings, which often meant crying, cursing, or screaming into my pillow, they started to dissipate. To my surprise, feelings won't kill you. It's the rejection of the heart that does the most harm.

- **Being whole *is* strong.** One of the toughest lessons I've learned during my healing journey is that I don't have to be strong *all the time*. It's not even possible, but I was an Oscar-winning actress when it came to faking as though I wasn't hurting and everything was all right. I think back to all the years I suffered in silence and became sick or anxious because of it, and I wish I had given myself grace sooner. When I allowed myself to be a whole person with a full range of complex emotions and needs, it gave me the strength and grounding necessary to go after my dreams, like writing this book.

Here are some additional tips to tap into your emotions and reconnect with your heart:

- **Seek therapy if you have access to it.** Resources like *Therapy for Black Girls*, an online space created by Dr. Joy

continued

Harden Bradford, gave me a list of culturally competent therapists in my area to choose from.

- **Journal your feelings.** Writing is an excellent way to get your emotions out without having to share them with someone else if you aren't ready. I keep journals in various sizes all around my house. I also invested in a digital writing tablet where I can archive my writings and organize them into folders like *Poetry* and *Bright Ideas* that I can easily find later.

Restore Your Body

One of the key revelations I've had throughout my healing journey is just how important the body is to sustain your efforts, to ground you in the present moment, and to be a barometer for when you're in need of care. In Chapter 4, I described how I went from being in the best shape of my life after serving in the United States Army Reserves to years later being hospitalized for a stress-related illness.

Like so many of us, I underestimated the limits of what my body could take and overlooked the fatigue, aches, intestinal issues, anemia, and overuse injuries that were signals of neglect. In this chapter, I described how I learned to dissociate from my body's needs in college. I was carrying a full course load, working nearly full-time to help pay for books and housing, and still trying to live a normal college life of late-night studying, parties, and hanging out with my then-boyfriend Al.

My propensity to burn the candle at both ends started in college but morphed into an unhealthy compulsion that powered most of my corporate career. I was determined to get ahead, and that meant working ten-plus-hour days, commuting two hours each way, and taking what felt like suicide missions to prove myself again and again at each step of the corporate ladder. All of this excessive work and stress resulted in numerous illnesses and hospital visits over the years until Al died, and I was forced to get back in tune with my body. The physical aspects of grief were so pronounced that I couldn't make it through the day without experiencing pain and fatigue. I eventually discovered yoga as a form of relief and stress management.

Here are some of the ways I **restored my body** and continue to ground myself:

- **Pay attention to your body's signals.** Your body will always show signs of equilibrium when everything is functioning properly and, conversely, will show signs of trouble. Stress and burnout often manifest physically with headaches, fatigue, insomnia, illness, and feelings of sadness or apathy. Any of these symptoms can occur by themselves; however, when you notice recurring or persistent physical issues, this is likely a sign you're overtaxing your body and need relief.

- **What you ignore in your mind or spirit shows up in the body.** For most of my career, I put myself in situations of immense stress and pressure to advance, along with constantly raising the bar with my own mental script of needing to work harder and be twice as good to succeed. And because of my family and cultural conditioning, I wouldn't admit to myself or others when the stress had gotten too much. Those difficult emotions and anxiety I thought I had buried emerged in the form of illness and dysfunction in various parts of my body.

- **Maintaining your body is the key to sustainable success.** I have stayed up till midnight many nights in my

continued

career, believing that if I could just get my email inbox to
zero or get a jump on that next project, work would be
easier that week. But what actually happened was that I
woke up too exhausted each day to function at my best,
and this snowballed into months and years of not enough
rest or relaxation, resulting in burnout. Once I began to
prioritize regular rest and movement and instilled healthy
work boundaries after returning from my bereavement
leave, I discovered that I'm far more productive and creative when I honor what my body needs.

In addition to the previous principles, I've found these tactics
particularly helpful:

- **Get regular movement**. Whether it's walking, yoga, or
  going to the gym, choose some form of movement you can
  perform most days of the week to keep your body functioning properly and help yourself manage daily stress.

- **Don't overdo it.** If you're an overachiever like me,
  even movement can become too much of a good thing
  when you treat it like a performance goal. Instead, find
  an activity you truly enjoy and see how you can naturally incorporate it into your week so it doesn't feel like
  a chore. I love to dance, so in the mornings, I usually
  put on a playlist and bust a move in my bedroom while
  getting ready for work. I see movement as medicine for
  my body, mind, and spirit and as a way to reconnect
  all three.

Reframe Your Beliefs

Like most people, my belief system is heavily influenced by how and where I grew up. In Chapter 5, I describe how growing up in an underserved community, raised by my Black parents, who had migrated to California from the rural South to escape segregation, shaped my values and perceptions of the world. Because of my parents' experiences of racism and knowing what challenges I would likely encounter as a little Black girl, they instilled in me the determination to work "twice as hard" to get ahead.

I heeded their advice all throughout school, excelling in both academics and extracurricular activities. I continued to outwork and overprepare when I entered the corporate workforce. I share in this chapter how I was programmed to overachieve and took on special job assignments as a means to get promoted. Most of these stretch assignments were added work that other colleagues weren't willing to do—or, frankly, didn't have to do—to get ahead. But in my case, these were critical for me to stand out from the crowd and "prove my worth," a song and dance I would have to repeat throughout my career, sadly.

I worked constantly. My work phone was attached to my hand like an appendage. I believed that if I didn't hustle or work twice as hard, I wouldn't get to the next level. I believed that if I could just show them what I was made of, they would see my worth. I believed that I had to be prepared and ready at all times, or people would think I was incompetent. These and many more beliefs made up the operating script that kept me on a perpetual hamster wheel of stress and exhaustion. Even when my father was diagnosed with cancer, I struggled to fully unplug and be present to care for him and my own emotional needs.

When Al died, it upended everything I thought I knew to be true about the world. That single event wiped out my hard drive, and I had to both reboot and install a whole new operating system to restart my life.

The following are some of the key lessons I learned that helped to **reframe my beliefs**:

- **Recognize when you're reacting versus choosing to act.** I consider myself to be action-oriented. At work, I was always quick to respond to requests because I wanted to be seen as being on top of things. But in reality, I was reacting to emotional triggers and limiting beliefs about what I needed to do to get ahead. Subconscious fears drove my behaviors instead of intentional choice. Now I can quickly recognize when I'm reacting, which is typically when I have an immediate compulsion to do something. When I catch myself with this urge, I stop and contemplate whether what I want to do is really necessary or if I'm doing it to be seen a certain way or please someone else. Sometimes I'll even wait an hour or a day to respond to that email or finish a task because it gives me time to assess my motives and ensure I'm making an active choice instead of responding on autopilot from pressure, guilt, or fear. I've come to realize that when I choose to act, I work with more ease, and the output is more thoughtful and creative.

- **Set solid boundaries; they will set you free.** For the majority of my career, I sincerely believed that I had to respond to every email, attend every meeting thrown on my calendar, and say yes to every assignment to perform my job well and advance my career. This belief kept me trapped in stressful jobs and situations that led to burnout. When I returned from bereavement leave, I had fresh eyes and a new outlook on life. Through therapy, meditation, journaling, movement, and reflection,

I reconnected with my true self. I learned to be more present and rely more on my inner wisdom than on my compulsive thoughts. This resulted in naturally setting better boundaries, such as not working on weekends, ending work by 5:00 p.m. most days, and focusing my time at work on the things that drove impact. These boundaries freed me up to disconnect and enjoy my nights and weekends and be present for family and friends. And contrary to my old beliefs, I performed even better at work because I felt rested, clear-minded, and fulfilled.

- **Master your to-do list with time-management techniques.** There are tons of workbooks, apps, and go-to books on time management, including *The 80/20 Principle* by Richard Koch or *The 7 Habits of Highly Effective People* by Stephen Covey. I've derived my own method, which I've dubbed "3D Time Ownership," to have agency over my daily workload (both personally and professionally), my team's project load, and requests for my time. Before I take action on anything that crosses my desk, I consider the following:

  ○ **Can I delete?** Is this something that needs to be done? Am I or my team the appropriate ones to do it?

  ○ **Can I defer?** Does it have to be done right now, or can it wait for a different day or time?

  ○ **Can I delegate?** Is there someone on my team who can do this, or someone else who is better equipped?

  If the answer to these three questions is "no," the item gets added to my to-do list.

Renew Your Spirit

Before my husband died, I was meandering through life on autopilot most days, doing what I was obligated to do or what I thought I was supposed to do instead of living for myself. To be honest, I had lost touch with who I really was behind the façade of my superwoman persona. I was buried beneath family responsibilities, work requirements, financial obligations, and societal expectations.

But when Al died, suddenly, all of the constraints that bound me like a straitjacket evaporated, and I was temporarily alone in the world. I don't mean alone in the physical sense; I was surrounded by loved ones. However, I was on a solo journey to rediscover my soul, which started in earnest when I decided to try group therapy.

I describe in Chapter 6 how group therapy, particularly the Grief Writing Workshop I attended, took me to the depths of my soul to examine the remnants of grief I had buried when I returned to everyday life following my bereavement. In this chapter, I also described how my regular hobby of listening to podcasts led me to discover Human Design, a spiritual modality for understanding how you're intended to operate in the world.

Then I shared how reconnecting with long-lost friends helped to remind me of who I was at my core before life took me in so many different directions. My girlfriends from high school came back into my life and surrounded me with love and laughter and rekindled a lightness in me that I hadn't felt since I was a teenager. Finally, I describe how a random hangout with friends led to me meeting an incredible man that blossomed into new love in my life.

Although I share a lot of details in this chapter, here are some additional methods you can try out to **renew your spirit**:

- **Be open to whatever comes your way.** Life has a way of surprising you . . . if you let it! My openness to going

out with friends and allowing the night to unfold naturally led to me finding love again when I least expected it.
I'm a true believer now in the saying, "Go with the flow."
Say yes more—especially to the things that electrify you,
intrigue you, or even scare you because they're outside of
your comfort zone.

- **Reconnect with childhood joy.** As a kid, I loved to read,
  I was passionate about dance, and I loved spending time
  with my friends. During my healing journey, I leaned
  into all of those things, and it renewed my spirit. Are
  there interests you had as a kid that you don't make time
  for anymore? Are there places you used to go that hold
  special memories or meaning? Children are more willing
  and able to freely indulge in what their hearts desire. I
  found that when I reconnected with my childhood joy, it
  helped to remind me of who I am at my core. Consider
  for yourself what activity, person, or place makes you feel
  happy and grounded.

- **Know thyself.** In addition to reconnecting with friends
  and past hobbies, I took time to go deeply inward to study
  myself. In Chapter 6, I described how grief writing was a
  wonderful modality for me to unearth buried emotions,
  which then accelerated my healing. I discovered Human
  Design, a spiritual framework that gave language to my
  unique makeup and lived experiences. I also explored
  the Enneagram assessment for more personal insight.
  There are countless tools and assessments on the market
  for self-discovery. Whichever you choose, use them as an
  opportunity to know yourself more deeply. It's only when
  you tap into your innate wisdom and desires that you can
  chart a course to more meaning and purpose.

Reinvent Your Routines

That first year after my husband passed away, I felt broken, and for a while, I was incapable of feeling anything at all. But as a testament to the human spirit, my instinct and intuition led me to keep searching for the light at the end of the tunnel.

In Chapter 7, I reveal the Pleasure Principles I learned over the course of my healing journey and now live by. The first principle, *Give yourself permission to indulge,* was born out of my decision to throw myself an extravagant birthday party, complete with dancers I hired to perform with me. I had so much fun and will always cherish the memory of celebrating how far I have come with those I love.

The second principle I shared is *Embrace new adventures.* The trip that my boyfriend and I took to Puerto Vallarta a few months after we met was largely spontaneous. Before my husband died, I was the type of person who had a plan and a contingency for that plan. But losing him loosened my grip and false sense of control, which made it easier to say yes to an incredible adventure.

I also discuss in this chapter the principle of *Saying many more nos to make space for the juicy yeses!* I love this principle, but I have to admit it was the hardest for me to implement. As a lifelong overachiever and people-pleaser, my life was full of things I "had" to do, with very few things I truly wanted to do. But once I tapped back into who I am at my core, it became clear what my real desires were.

The final eye-opener for me was going through a round of interviews at another company that helped me realize I was no longer passionate about my work. I had a deep calling to share my life lessons to help other women, particularly women of color, avoid the pitfalls and pain I experienced. This epiphany reignited my childhood dream of writing a book. Thank goodness I said no to more of the same so I could make space for my true purpose to manifest!

In Chapter 7, I outlined several tips and tactics to put these pleasure principles into practice. For every principle, I shared examples of what you can do to implement these in your life. These tactics range from small things like treating yourself to coffee or your favorite beverage to bigger shifts like the "no responsibility for twenty-four hours" rule that has given me more freedom and ease amid a busy life. As I stated in the chapter, it's not lost on me that I had the financial means and circumstances to indulge myself more than many people can. However, I'd encourage you to find ways to add more joy, rest, and fun to your life within your own budget.

Here are two **low-/no-cost ideas** for living more fully:

- **Create a drugstore spa day.** The next time you visit your neighborhood drugstore or discount retailer, check out the beauty section for discounts or even travel-size products for bath and body. When I've had a rough week, I'll go to the local drugstore and purchase a moisturizing face mask, pedicure socks, and my favorite magazine. And then I go home and enjoy my at-home spa for less than twenty dollars!

- **Explore free local attractions.** Research places to go in your area with free admission. When my son was little, we were barely surviving and living paycheck to paycheck, but we still found ways to have fun. I love museums, so we would visit them on free or reduced admission days. One of our best family outings was a free trip to the Cable Car Museum in San Francisco.

No matter what you choose to do, it's important to find ways to incorporate your favorite practices into your regular routine so you can sustain your newfound Zen for the long run.

Finding Home

There have been times in my life when I've felt like I'm in a dream-like state, untethered from reality or time. These have been times of great transition or extraordinary circumstances. Moving from East Palo Alto to Livermore was one instance. The birth of my son, Morgan, felt surreal. Losing Al knocked my world off its axis. And for some reason, waking up on the tiny island of St. Thomas in the US Virgin Islands that July morning in 2022 felt like I had arrived on the moon.

It wasn't that St. Thomas itself was strange. It's a beautiful Caribbean island full of vibrant culture, hardworking people, and deep history. What was different for me was waking up in sheer bliss after having survived life's chaos the prior year. The time between May 2021, when Al died, to July 5, 2022, when I woke up with the fresh, tropical sun peeking through the blue-and-white curtains of the bedroom window, was a chasm of sorrow, loss, bargaining, apathy, acceptance, and finally peace.

Jeff and I had been dating for seven months, and our relationship was going great. Each date or weekend trip seemed to deepen our bond, although when we met, I already felt as though I knew him on an instinctive level. St. Thomas would be the first time we'd be together for a full week. But I wasn't worried. Anytime we were together, we vibed, and things just naturally clicked.

On this particular morning, we were scheduled to go to one of those timeshare presentations at our resort, where they hold you in a tiny room with stale pastries and talk ad nauseam about the "hidden benefits of timeshare ownership." All while they aggressively pressure you to sign away your life's savings for an off-season week in Mexico. I, for one, wasn't falling for it. When Al and I were newly married, we purchased a timeshare we could barely afford. Therefore, I knew their sales tactics very well. Luckily for us, though, my parents were the timeshare owners who gifted us the trip. And because we weren't the actual owners, we were told right before the presentation started that we didn't have to attend. Thank you, Mom and Dad, for the amazing trip and for the perfect exit strategy!

Seizing our newfound freedom, Jeff and I decided to go to the resort's front office to speak to the concierge about possible activities for us to do that morning. The short walk from the timeshare presentation up the hill to the front desk was a tropical nature walk. We spotted an iguana climbing down a tree near the pool. We encountered some geese sauntering down our trail. The warm, eighty-degree weather was heavenly. It was the perfect temperature for the short white sundress I was wearing. Jeff was dressed for the climate, too, with a teal green shirt that read "Stress Free" and some tropical shorts to match.

We arrived in the lobby of the resort and were immediately greeted by the air-conditioned breeze and a delightful aroma of whatever cleaning products had been recently applied. We let the front desk receptionist know that we wanted to see the concierge. She offered us some water and asked us to have a seat while she gave him a call.

Jeff and I were greeted by a familiar face, Ty, who was the concierge present when we checked in the day before. Ty was a chocolate-skinned man with a connecting mustache and beard that framed his round face. He had gentle eyes with the depth of someone who has seen the best and worst that life has to offer. He had bowed legs and walked with a slight hitch due to his knees—although he attributed his most recent knee pain to dropping it too low at St. John's Carnival over the weekend.

After we greeted each other, the three of us easily dove into a conversation like we were old friends sitting around a kitchen table. Ty began to tell us the story of how he arrived in the Virgin Islands. He was originally from the States and had visited St. Thomas for the first time in 2014. During that trip, while he was having dinner with his partner, he had an epiphany. *I could move here*, he thought to himself. When he got back home, he started to research everything he could about the island.

Ty shared that he returned to St. Thomas in 2020 for a visit. He said that as soon as he got off the plane, he had this feeling. He proceeded to go to his cousin's house, who lived in nearby St. John, so he could drop off his stuff before hitting the beach. As soon as he got into the waters of Trunk Bay, he heard a voice say, "You're Home."

Ty returned to his cousin's house that afternoon, where he learned that his uncle had been researching their family's lineage and discovered they had more family on the island. He was able to trace his family's roots from the Virgin Islands to South Carolina via the Transatlantic Slave Trade. Ty decided then to relocate to St. Thomas, as he had indeed found home.

Ty's story gave me chills. In that instance, I could imagine him stepping into the warm waters of the Caribbean and being beautifully held by the love and legacy of his ancestors. At one point, he shared with us that he, too, had been through a devastating tragedy, and being here in St. Thomas was part of his healing journey.

Ty's revelation pierced my soul because I felt like St. Thomas was a destination on my journey to revive my spirit. This trip symbolized rest, freedom, adventure, new beginnings, and in many ways, similar to Ty, a **return home**—a return to an unencumbered version of myself that I hadn't experienced since I was a little girl.

The trip to St. Thomas was a tipping point for me. Before that, I had been test-driving joy through new hobbies, solo trips, and minor indulgences during the week. I had been trying happiness on for size like I would a coat I might purchase if I could find the perfect fit. But being in St. Thomas, a world away from my everyday life, gave me a glimpse of the life I wanted in the future. A life of adventure, freedom, joy, and peace that I could have even after I returned home.

Do You

I've learned so many valuable lessons along my healing journey that are embedded in the personal stories within this book. But one lesson stands out above the rest. It's the one that Al made sure he imparted before he crossed over . . .

In the initial aftermath of Al's death, I couldn't even look at his picture without welling up in tears. For months I didn't even touch his belongings, preferring instead to wall them off in his closet—a feeble attempt to keep the memories at bay.

But one day, sometime in the fall of 2021, I had the urge to go through my pictures and find every single one I had of Al. This quickly became a compulsion to capture every image of him for fear of his likeness fading out of my mind's eye.

The mission then turned from finding every picture to mining all forms of media for voicemails, videos, and text messages. I wanted any remnants left of my husband here on Earth. I had some luck finding some special pictures and clips I had forgotten about. But I couldn't access the pictures on his phone. He had a biometric password, and I never wrote down the numeric code he had shared with me. I had no choice but to abandon that dead end, at least temporarily.

Then something whispered to me to check my text messages for the last message he sent me. I opened my phone and went to our text thread and saw he had sent me two images the night before he died, one of me and one of him sitting across from me at dinner. He had texted me those pics during dinner, so those weren't a surprise. What I discovered, though, took my breath away.

The last text message he wrote to me read:

Do you, babe. Don't worry about anything else.

I instantly teared up. I reread the message again and again, taking it into every cell of my body. These were my husband's last wishes for me. I was so grateful to have it documented. But it didn't seem like enough to have found the text message and saved it. Al had left me sacred instructions that I wanted to honor going forward. After much thought, I decided to get these words tattooed on the inside of my left forearm as an eternal reminder to follow my heart.

About a year after I had gotten the tattoo, I discovered its true meaning.

It was nearing the end of 2022, and I was in the initial stages of writing this book. As I was writing my outline for Chapter 1, reminiscing on that stressful day that I joined Adam Mosseri for my first IG Live as head of DEI, a flashback stopped me in my tracks. As I recalled the events of that IG Live on May 21, something told me to check the date and time of Al's last text message.

Sure enough, his text message was on the morning of my big event! I was blown away. As I reflected on the timing of his message some more, it gave me chills. Yes, Al sent that text message to encourage me before that particular event. Yet it ended up being the last thing he expressed to me because he was too sick to talk by the time he was rushed to the hospital the day he died. I'm not a believer in coincidence. I believe his soul knew he was nearing the end of his time on Earth and wanted to impart this final gift—a message to remain true to myself no matter what.

To this day, in times of stress and uncertainty, I look down at the tattoo on my left arm and find courage in those words. There were so many days after he passed that I felt abandoned. But before he departed the physical realm, Al left me with a compass in the form of a message to help me find my way home.

Epilogue

As you've seen throughout this book, my life has unfolded in some beautiful and devastating ways. I followed the blueprint for success but lost myself in the process. **I now know there is a better way**—a way to lead a more meaningful life that I've outlined within these pages.

If you've found yourself reading this book, something has been whispering in you, and you're already on the right path. **Keep going**. Keep seeking. Keep learning. Keep reflecting. Keep evolving. Keep loving.

Life is never easy, but the journey is worth it. I've grown more in the last two years since my husband died than I could have ever imagined. It's funny how the universe always guides us toward a bigger vision—a destiny we could have never fully dreamed of for ourselves.

You will traverse many peaks and valleys on your journey. Sometimes you will fail. At other times you will go astray.

But it is never too late to pivot, to start anew, to recommit, or to discover your true purpose.

You were divinely created to uniquely impact the world.

You are meant to live a meaningful life if you're willing to commit to it. Never stop trying.

And if all else fails, simply **do you**. I promise you won't regret it.

Acknowledgments

It seems unfathomable that I would be sitting here writing acknowledgments for a book I always knew I'd write (although I wasn't certain of the subject matter) without the person I was accustomed to doing everything with.

Al, this is for you, my dearest. Without you, I wouldn't have had the courage to pursue my dreams, albeit deferred. It was you who taught me my two greatest lessons in this life—the meaning of love and the devastation of loss. Thank you for twenty-one incredible years and helping me raise our bright and beautiful son. Our love endures in this realm and beyond.

To Morgan—in many ways, I wrote this book for you too. I know you have your own experience of losing your dad. But I hope through my version of events and the other stories I've shared in the book, that you'll see the picture more fully. I pray you'll feel the magnitude of not only what we lost but that you also take comfort in the courage it took for all of us to keep going. This period in your life may be the hardest thing you'll ever go through. No matter what comes your way, these months and years are evidence of your resilience and how deeply you are loved.

This entire journey started with my parents. Thank you for working so hard to provide a better life for us. You were my first example of love and sacrifice, of hard times and grit, of hope and the American Dream. Your words of wisdom, tough lessons, and nurturing presence gave me an incredible foundation to build from. You have always been in my corner, even when you disagree with my choices. Thank you for instilling in me that I could be anything in the world I wanted if I worked hard enough.

I am forever grateful to my brother Mark and his wife, Angel. You were the first people I called when I woke up disoriented the morning after Al died. You stayed on the phone and lovingly held space as I cried uncontrollably, unsure of how to go on. You surrounded me with much-needed love and support when I came down to visit you that first summer after Al passed, which I remain thankful for. And Mark, you will always be my big (tall) little brother. You were my day one and always will be. I love you beyond words.

To my forever "little sister" Keandra. Although we didn't grow up together because of our age difference I always felt we had a special bond. And over the last two years, that bond has grown exponentially. You came to live with me at the lowest point in my life and helped me not only function again but find laughter, companionship, and purpose again. Thank you for all you've done to support me and Morgan throughout this period. I'm so honored to bear witness to your personal growth during this time as well as to the beautiful, vibrant woman you have become. I love and appreciate you more than you know.

To all my other family and friends who showed up, showed care, and provided food, hugs, flowers, words of wisdom, love, and any and all forms of support, I feel so blessed to have you in my and my son's life. Thank you for holding us up and loving us back to life. And I would be remiss not to mention another source of unconditional love, my adorable dog, Rocket. I'm thankful to him for getting me out of bed each day and, quite literally, keeping me going.

To my friends and former colleagues at Meta, thank you for showing me so much respect and care following Al's death. You called, texted, arranged a recurring delivery of sympathy cards, sent flowers, and donated enough Door Dash credits to provide Morgan and me with dinner for months. I am truly humbled by your kindness. From day one, I felt welcomed by the DEI team and fully embraced by the Instagram Org. Meta is the capstone of my corporate career and perhaps the place I've grown the most, professionally and personally. Thank you for the ride of a lifetime.

To my fabulous book coach, Stacy Ennis. Without your expertise and consistent guidance, this book would not have come to life in this magnificent form. You saw my vision and helped it take shape and were my sounding board as I struggled to pour my pain and joy into every word on the page. Thank you for your encouragement, accountability, and artful touches along the way. And to your dear friend and mine, Misty Megia. Thank you, Misty, for introducing me to Stacy and for being an amazing neighbor to Al and me and a terrific mentor, supporter, and friend.

To my publisher, Greenleaf Book Group, thank you for recognizing the potential this book had in the very beginning to heal hearts and open minds. You have held my hand every step of the way, making a lengthy, sometimes emotional process feel seamless. Thank you for helping to bring my dream of being an author to life.

To my surprise love, Jeff. You have taught me the most interesting lessons about life. From you, I learned that love comes within its own timeframe and in its own rhythm. When I least expected to find someone, there you were with a deeply kind yet tentative heart like mine—recovering from heartache. Together we found peace. Together we found comfort. Together we found a blissful kind of love that is whole and exuberant, a love that is triumphant and only arrives in the wake of the ashes. Thank you, baby, for all that you are and continue to be in my life.

And lastly, thank YOU for reading my story. For all the people who find themselves lost at some point or another in this life, I hope this book gives you a blueprint and some hope to continue your journey. Although your life's compass may seem off course, trust your intuition to find your way. I did, and the view from here is glorious.

About the Author

REGINA LAWLESS, MSOD, is an author, leadership coach, and former head of diversity, equity, and inclusion (DEI) at Instagram. In addition, Regina is the founder and CEO of *Bossy & Blissful*, a membership community for high-achieving Black women to connect, recharge, and reprioritize their well-being.

Regina has eighteen-plus years of HR experience working for Fortune 500 companies across various industries, including Target, Safeway (Albertsons), and Intel. Prior to Instagram and Meta, she served as the global director of diversity, equality, and inclusion at Micron Technology, where she led the creation of their diversity curriculum and spearheaded talent initiatives to mitigate bias in interviews and performance discussions.

Regina spent the early part of her career as an HR business partner, working closely with business leaders to translate their goals into effective people strategies. With the desire to have greater impact, she decided to pursue specialized roles in organizational development (OD), learning and development, and diversity, equity, and inclusion.

DEI is the culmination of her varied HR experience and personal passion for social justice that was fostered at an early age. Regina grew up in an underserved community that bordered some of the most affluent zip codes in the country. Experiencing inequality firsthand has made her determined to work toward creating equal opportunity in the workplace and the world.

In 2021, Regina was appointed to the Board of the World Women Foundation and serves as an Advisory Council Member for the University of San Francisco's Engineering Program. She is a graduate of California State University, Sacramento, in Communication Studies and holds a Master of Science degree in Organization Development from the University of San Francisco. Regina is a Bay Area native and currently resides there with her partner, Jeff; her son; and their dog, Rocket. She is an avid reader who loves listening to music and podcasts and practicing yoga.